ADDICTED TO LIES

ADDICTED TO LIES

TERRELL PATTERSON

purposely
created
PUBLISHING

ADDICTED TO LIES

Published by Purposely Created Publishing Group™

Copyright © 2017 Terrell Patterson

All rights reserved.

Scriptures marked NIV are taken from the New International Version®. Copyright © 1973, 1978, 1984, 2011 by Biblica, Inc.™ All rights reserved.

Printed in the United States of America

ISBN: 978-1-945558-38-2

Special discounts are available on bulk quantity purchases by book clubs, associations, and special interest groups. For details email:
sales@publishyourgift.com
or call (888) 949-6228.

For information logon to:
www.PublishYourGift.com

CONTENTS

INTRODUCTION

STOP LYING TO YOURSELF.

You're probably saying to yourself, "Well, I've heard this typical phrase before. What's the big deal about it?"

Have you ever thought about how lying to yourself can actually cause a domino effect that will play a major part not only in your life, but also in the lives of billions of who will encounter your damaged behavior? Every life and condition starts somewhere, just as God said in Genesis 1:27, "So God created mankind in his own image, in the image of God he created them; male and female he created them." Even though we can't fully handcraft other human beings as the Creator does, we still have enough power to create major ripples from ourselves that affect other people's lives, mentally, physically, emotionally or psychologically. Now, you might not study the Bible or have a full relationship with Jesus Christ, but God is so awesome that He will not deny you the power to alter your life, as well as other people's lives for the better, hopefully in a direction that leads to Him.

THE DOMINO EFFECT

Dom·i·no ef·fect:
A domino effect is the cumulative effect produced when one event sets off a chain of similar events. The term is best known as a mechanical effect and is used as an analogy to a falling row of dominoes. It typically refers to a link sequence of events where the time between successive events is relatively small.

DOMINO 1

THE SEED OF LIES

In my childhood, I encountered many emotional ups and downs, good times and bad times. I grew up in Baltimore City and, for the most part, I lived in either a neighborhood infested with drugs or saturated with violence. Regardless of where I lived, it was always busy, people moving up and down the street whether it was a weekday or weekend, night or day—time seemed irrelevant to everyone.

How a person spends his or her life as a baby to a toddler then up to a teenager sets up the "domino effect" of that individual's future. For instance, my biological father who had an unhappy childhood and rebellious teenage lifestyle, eventually ended up in prison with a sixty-seven-year sentence. He had been a great blocking fullback football player in high school and worked himself up to playing as a semi-pro. But after realizing that he wasn't going to the pros, he decided by any means necessary to take care of himself and his family. Most of his childhood buddies were bad company, but he kept his loyalty to them, even when they didn't return him the same courtesy. He was a leader, yet still allowed himself to be lowered into peer pressure by devilish acts such as selling drugs, robbing people and stores, and even using guns whenever he felt was necessary for the job. However, I always was told that, though he had a quick temper, he was never physical or verbally abusive towards my mother during the short time they were together—he was only territorial over us.

As for my mother, she was that beautiful five-foot three-inch lady who always dressed fly and kept her appearance up to date, even if her private life wasn't great. My father used to either be quick to knock dudes out or even pull out guns on them if they dared approach her. From all the stories I've heard of my mother's younger days, guys were instantly attracted to her, but just couldn't get up the courage to say anything. It wasn't just fear of my father, but because she kept that serious "You better come correct or not at all" demeanor.

She and my father were only seventeen and eighteen years of age, respectively, when I was born; he was sentenced to all that prison time when I was three years old, and the hurt pushed her in the direction of a carefree lifestyle that sometimes made her forgo her parental responsibilities. As years went by and I grew older, I was constantly bouncing from one house to the next, even being left on family members' door steps after my mother told me that she would return shortly.

She often would say, "I am going around the corner to the store and will be right back. What do you want me to get you?" and I would ask for "ice cream with bumps on it" (aka strawberry shortcake ice cream).

She would return with whatever I asked her for, only three to five months would have passed by then. It's funny now, but that abandonment and series of lies truly did scar me, because, for the life of me, I couldn't understand why the woman who birthed me, the woman I should receive constant love from, would not want to be with me or habitually tell lies that I accepted, even when I knew they weren't true. I learned about my mother and father, mainly from relatives and friends, so basically everybody else that surrounded me played daddy and mommy roles to raise me.

DOMINO II

REVERSED ROLES

Neither of my parents were there for the highlights of my life: They missed my elementary, middle and even high school graduations. Actually, my grandfather, who I was living with at the time, picked up my mother so that she could at least witness the very end of my high school graduation, which was an awkward but grateful experience. But overall, it hurt like hell to have successful moments that very few in my immediate family had achieved, only to be met with two empty seats in the crowd.

A year after my final graduation, when I turned nineteen-years-old, my mother revealed to me that she was sick and was diagnosed with HIV from sharing needles while using drugs. I also found out she was raped a few years prior while dating an ex-drug "king pin." Deep inside me, there was love for her that had been overshadowed by hurt, betrayal, and bitterness; I decided to take care of her through that darkest moment of life. I aided her for the next three years, but she still had moments of lying and even stealing things inside our apartment, whether it was food from the fridge or a $1,300 marble top dining room table. I did my best to keep my composure, to understand that my mother was going through withdrawals and an illness that caused her to relapse back to this sort of behavior.

Eventually, after enrolling my mother in three different drug rehab programs including the last one in Philadelphia, PA, she stopped using drugs and never turned back. With a clear system, she made a decision to accept Jesus Christ as her savior. After that, she went on to assist over two hundred drug users get help for their addiction. After a while, she and I developed a close relationship: She became one of my best friends, but more importantly, she continues to be my hero, because of her courage to fight and her faith that God was going to cure her.

I can still hear that thundering voice coming from that frail body of hers, the boldness she had that day in the hospital, looking the doctor straight in his eyes. A force of determination spoke out as she said to him, "I'm not going to die. Only my God will make that decision—not you!" He had just told her that she had three months to live. But after the third, the same doctor slowly walked into the room, shaking his head with astonishment.

"Ma'am, I don't know what God you serve, but don't stop serving Him," he said. "Because, for the first time in my career, I had met someone diagnosed with HIV and without Magic Johnson's money, whose illness has become completely undetectable. Gone."

Believe it or not, that was eleven years ago, and my mother is still alive—Praise God!

Even though I had forgiven my mother and father, the domino effect didn't stop the wave that was already put into motion in my life. My father eventually was released from prison in 2006 after twenty-five years of time served and good behavior during his sentence, the year my first daughter was born. I hoped that he would've given her time that he missed out on with me, but his past life grabbed a hold of him again, distracting the grandfather he was supposed to be to her and the father he was supposed to be to me.

DOMINO III

IMMATURE LOVE

When I was around seventeen or eighteen-years-old, I had my first "in-love" moment. I was reintroduced to a girl who I first met at my elementary school: Her name was Deidra and I didn't pay that much attention to her in school, but did remember she was always dressed neatly in a color-coordinated styles from her hair barrettes down to her shoe strings, reminding me of my mother's matching dress style. We met again through a mutual girl friend, who attended elementary school with us. They were best friends but, before I found out, I was already interested in dating the friend, Desire. I was attracted to her because she lived in our neighborhood, yet still handled herself more ladylike than other women that were around. Desire's mother, Denise or Niecy as we called her, used to love me so much because, though she knew or heard that I was a "hoodlum," I always showed respect and manners in adult presence.

One day, Desire had Deidra stay the weekend with

her. After Deidra and I talked for almost four hours on Desire's porch on Friday night, I started noticing the way our vibes matched. She laughed at all my jokes, and I remember how my uncle used to tell me, "You found a good one, if she laughs at your jokes. Especially if they aren't that funny." Around eight at night I had to leave, but I told her I would come back if she wanted me to. She asked me to promise that I would come back. After being lied to all my life, I didn't want her feeling the same disappointment, so I responded, "Just believe me. I'll be back."

I made it back to keep my word to her, not only that evening but on Saturday and Sunday, too. We stayed on the porch talking and laughing until midnight and sometimes later, and I shared my life story with her.

When the weekend came to an end, she told me she had to leave once her mother came to pick her up. Once again, I felt like another woman I've gotten close to and now trusted was rolling out on me, just as my mom did. Selfish and caught up in my feelings, I didn't go that Sunday evening to see her off. She eventually called my grandparent's home, leaving messages saying that she would be leaving around 6:30 pm. I asked myself over and over, "How can I convince her to come back again?"

Right then, all the macho-ism that I had known went out the window. I grabbed the biggest stuffed animal I ever won shooting hoops at Six Flags and ran as fast as I could through my neighborhood to catch her.

My buddies laughed and made jokes, yet I was too determined to make it before she left, just in time as her mother was pulling up in a taxi. That day, I realized I had reached an emotional level that I didn't think existed in me. I walked up to the taxi and gave Deidra the gift as a token of how I felt. Even though her mother looked suspicious, I was too focused on Deidra, standing there and smiling with amazement.

From then on, we talked constantly as if we were still on that porch, but after the first month, the physical distance between us became overwhelming and I felt slightly abandoned. She lived about twenty minutes away, but being that I didn't have a car, I would ride the subway all the way downtown and then jump on the bus, which extended my travel time to an hour. The visits slowed down from not always having the money for subway, buses, or taxi cab rides to see her, and our phone calls dwindled down. I eventually figured that, before I feel that hurt my mother left me with, I would just avoid her calls all together. For a time period, that actually worked and I was back outside, and three months had passed without thought: Summer break had come around and there was no more school—the fun had just begun for me and my homeboys in the neighborhood.

The first thing on the agenda was go to the summer jam backyard cookout party at Ms. Niecy and Desire's house. When I got there, guess who I ran into? Deidra. She was so excited to see me as if I didn't just kick her to the curb—no lost emotions, exactly how I was when my mother would just pop up after months went by. Instantly my mind went into lying mode, trying to think of every excuse to give her of my absence from her, though she never asked for one. We talked and danced as if nothing had happened within the last three months, and I even got in a fight with a guy at the party for just trying to get her phone number. My ego had me tripping, thinking, "He knows that she is my lady and is disrespecting me by asking for her number."

It's funny, because that same territorial demeanor would trigger my father's anger whenever someone approached my mother. Needless to say, the emotions grew deeper after that, because for the rest of summer break, Deidra and I were inseparable, talking exactly how we used to and kissing all night. It was like an addiction, and even when I went home on late nights, we still stayed on the phone, falling in and out of sleep together.

But when summer vacation was over, Deidra, once again, had to go back home; only this time, she explained how hurt she was the last time apart since the communication had stopped. Afterwards, she told me to promise her that we would keep in touch on a regular. That's just how I used to ask my mother to promise coming back. So, I didn't make any promises and instead said, "Girl, I ain't going nowhere." Soon after the first week of her leaving, I pushed her aside again through the same defense mechanism. This time hurt worse for me, and yet, my pride and generational habits wouldn't allow me to reach out and rekindle our hope for the future.

DOMINO IV

UNEXPECTED HURT

I started focusing on football and my senior homecoming was about to take place. The night before, I was so excited I couldn't sit still. I decided to play basketball out back in the alley with a couple of buddies including my best friend since pre-k, Johnathan Wilson aka J-Roc. Near the end of our b-ball game, I got injured from an elbow to the side of my head (that's how aggressive we played), so the game ended. I talked to J-Roc for about fifteen minutes afterwards about how he was definitely coming to my school, Forest Park High, to watch me play our homecoming football game. We even plotted how I was going to keep a side door to the school open so he could watch our prep rally in the gymnasium. I really wanted to go around the corner with him to chill out and finish our game plan for tomorrow, but he reminded me that I should go put ice on my head from that elbow hit. After laughing about it, we departed ways but not before he turned in my direction to say, "Man I'll definitely be with you tomorrow. That's my word." Then, right as he turned back around, he said, "Relly, love you, bro. See you tomorrow."

At first, that seemed a little weird because it's not often I heard or even told anyone that I love them except for my mother or grandmothers. Regardless, I responded back, "Love you, too, bro." I walked in the house and around the corner he went.

It was getting late in the evening. I was distracted by a call from a girl I was interested in, when I heard *Boom, boom, boom!* Multiple gunshots rang out from the direction where my homeboys said they were going to chill out. I paused, hoping the noise wasn't what I thought it was, but a couple minutes later, police and ambulance sirens came racing to that same direction. Three knocks came at the front door with someone yelling in a frantic voice, *"Relly!"* I ran to the door and another neighborhood buddy confirmed that the shooting did come from around the corner and someone had been shot. I raced around the corner, heart pounding, hoping that it was just a mistake. When I got to the scene, I could see that my cousin Greg aka G-money was shot once and another person was dead from multiple gunshots. I froze in my place when I saw that it was my childhood friend J-Roc. I tried to keep from crying in front of everyone; my uncle always said, "If you cry, the streets are going think you a punk," so I faked like it had no major impact on my emotions, until I walked a block away. The hurt imploded in me. I busted out windows, until Bo (an older neighborhood homeboy) grabbed me until I calmed down.

Overwhelmed with pain and frustration, selfishly, I thought about how he had made a promise that he would be at my game, the same day of telling me "I love you," and he was now gone. I felt hopeless, thinking how love constantly runs away from me. I questioned whether love even existed for me at all. Many folks came to check on me and reached out to show their support, including Deidra, but the numbness created a hardened heart in me. Almost two years went by where I didn't trust anyone to get close, so nobody even had a chance to be consistent and loyal in my life, including those I knew wouldn't have ever disappointed me. I was convinced that as long as I didn't allow an emotional bond to grow between folks and myself, than I couldn't get as hurt as I had been before.

DOMINO V

VULNERABLE ATTRACTIONS

One day, while working a part-time job at an electronics and music store called Metro 2, a woman asked me to help her find a record album for her brother's upcoming birthday party. We didn't have that particular album she needed, so I checked our other location to get it shipped to our store and told her that if she left her phone number with me, and I could call her when it arrived. What I can't lie about was that Miss Lady had caught my attention beyond the customer/sales clerk interaction. Her hair was in a well-pressed, elegant, down-style wrap, and she had a beautiful light caramel-toned face with lavender colored contact lenses. Yes, a black woman with lavender eyes! But I was most impressed by her smile.

I have always been a fan of ladies with fashionable style, which always reminded me of how neatly and put-together my mother used to dress. I could also tell by the woman's conversation that she had me by a few years. That weekend, the album she requested wasn't delivered, so I called to let her know, but my nerves got the best of me, as I thought to myself, "Now, what would this mature, grown woman want to do with a twenty-year-old?" My finances were probably chump change compared to hers and the slogan "Don't no woman want a man who they have to take care of" played on my mind. Recapping that thought in my head with her phone number in my hand, I couldn't imagine someone of her caliber not already married or at least engaged. Don't get me wrong: Even as a youngster, I had great confidence of the young man I was becoming, but this was no ordinary chick to add to my roster—this was a woman.

I got off work and explained everything to my homeboy Jamel aka Ugg and two other buddies, and they encouraged me to call her. They also made comments about how they never saw me intimidated by a woman, which struck a nerve in my ego. I thought to myself, "What's the worst that could happen?" I dialed the number, but only let the phone ring twice before I quickly hung up. I made up all types of excuses, including, "Maybe it's a sign that she didn't answer! At least I tried." No more than five minutes had passed by and her number popped up on the caller ID, and my heart started pounding faster than Jeff Gordon's race car.

Thinking of what I was going to say, I decided to start off the conversation about the record album she ordered and just to wing it from there. I answered the phone then reminded her who I was, and she responded in a surprised, yet excited voice, saying "Hey!" I explained to her that the album had not arrived as planned, which turned out to be fine since her brother had already found it elsewhere. I let her know how relieved I was, and for about five seconds, I was at a loss for words, as I thought to myself, "I learned how to pick up chicks but never was I taught what to do when approaching a woman." So, I ended the call, saying "Well, alright. You got my number if you need anything." The fellas and I know that's the most cowardly line to say, but I hoped that she would capitalize on the moment. She seemed unsure of wanting to hang up, but the door of opportunity slowly closed as we said our goodbyes before ending the call.

After feeling like a punk and getting joked on by my friends, I eventually mustered up the courage, put on my determined face, and called her back, even though I still didn't know exactly what to say. She answered the phone on the second ring, yet again that excited greeting, and without hesitation, I asked said straight to the point, "Are you married? I mean no disrespect if you are, but if not, I was wondering if I could take you out on a date one day soon." Yes, I used an old pick up line I remembered watching *Martin*. She paused, leaving me in absolute suspense. Then, uneasily, she responded, "Yes, I am married." As soon she said yes, my pride went straight into defense mode to guard my heart, the same tactic that I used after my mother rejected me. Then, she continued, "But I am in the process of separation."

Since my defense mode had already gone up, it took me a minute to realize she really didn't shut my attempt down. At that point, I didn't know exactly what to say to her last response even though the selfish part of me was relieved with that answer. I'm not sure where the confidence came from, but I repeated my offer, and she replied, "Sure, maybe we can even hook up this week-end." I instantly felt a level of confidence I had never experienced before. I was so on cloud nine that you couldn't tell me that, if I reached up, I wasn't going to touch an airplane.

My experience seeing men and women interacting was close to none, so while getting the date was fine, I was now stuck with the question of where to take a woman out for date night. I sat through that entire day, thinking if there were any men throughout the years of my life who would be a good example or I could go to for advice on my situation. My grandparents were the best examples, but I felt they were too old to relate, and all other possible candidates were single. The single ones embraced every bit of a carefree lifestyle and other couples I remembered only stayed together for their addiction to drugs. But later that day, an elderly man said to me, "Young brother, you got an old soul that's running a race with the older folks and two steps ahead of yours, but you have to start realizing what you do have a lot to offer and stop thinking of what you don't." It made me reflect on my young, conniving methods of dating chicks around my age; if I wanted this woman, I only had one shot to prove that I, while being younger, had to be taken as seriously as men her age. I knew our worlds were totally opposite, so I tried my best not to overwhelm her with my street mentality.

It was good I somewhat had my own apartment. I say "somewhat" because my mother was always running in and out, battling her drug addiction. Some days she would come home, then other times, it would be a week or two before I saw her again. Due to her illness, she qualified for permanent disability and received living assistance, but was still not capable of living by herself. At the time, my grandparents and I were only one's willing to take on that physical responsibility, making sure she kept her appointments and took her twelve medications every six hours. Other folks were scared of coming home to find their personal belongings stolen or sold. After they silently declined to help her, I decided at nineteen-years-old that I had to at least take on the challenge of taking care of her on my own. On the bright side, the situation benefitted the both of us: My mother could get her medication and go to her doctor appointments on time while I got a place that was basically like my own.

So back to the story: The woman, whose name was Lisa, finally called, and we talked for a little while on the phone before I asked to have our next conversation face-to-face. She replied, "Where are you going to be tomorrow around noon? I'll be on my lunch break so maybe I can stop by for a second." I agreed. I was so excited and nervous about making a strong impression that I ironed three different shirts without knowing. I went from feeling almost rejected to now meeting her at my place. Until it was time, I did what every guy does before a first meet: I stood in front of the mirror, rehearsing conversation lines, pretending my reflection was her.

It was about 12:10 pm and, sure enough, she pulled up outside my apartment complex, driving a smoke grey Toyota Camry with dark tinted windows. My confidence mode kicked in and I chose to greet her in the parking lot to assure her that I was not a typical guy who just wanted her there for sex. Everything went smooth with our conversation including a few laughs, and, thanks to being raised around older folks twice my age, I held an intellectual conversation, which surprised her. She soon shared with me that she and her husband had a three-year-old daughter who she would be keeping with her majority of the time once she was legally separated.

Our time was coming to an end, she reached out to give me a hug before getting into in her car, smiling with that beautiful smile I adored, and I tried hard to not seem "pressed." No more than ten minutes after pulling off, she called me to express how much she enjoyed the talk, how it went better than she expected, and how the fragrance I wore was still lingering inside her car. I tooted my own horn, yet still in the back of my mind, I was in the dark about the true connection she might have with her husband and the harsh reality that she was still married.

With very few responsible adults around me, I was clueless as to how I should deal with a situation like this. It also didn't help that she didn't allow her husband to interrupt our late night conversations for hours after putting her daughter to bed. Through that week, we talked consistently on the phone for hours throughout the day, including at work (she was a pre-k schoolteacher and we talked during nap time). I tried holding back the emotions that were rapidly growing, so I did everything in my power to compose myself, making sure to not seem dramatic.

DOMINO VI

ANOTHER MAN'S TREASURE

The strength to hold back changed us both after, one day, Lisa came over for her usual lunch break. Our time was winding down and she turned around for that departure hug, and out of the blue, I got the urge to kiss her softly on her neck causing a slight moan from her, that ended up with us on floor, making out. It was an amazing moment, but it also left me slightly confused because it wasn't the way I imagined how it was going to happened; I didn't expect a woman of her caliber to allow me to make love the same way as I had done with other chicks. From television, I thought that I needed silk sheets, bubble baths, Avant's "Read Your Mind" playing in the background, rose peddles covering the floor, etc. Either way, this was an incredible experience with a mature woman.

It was obvious that that moment enhanced her feelings for me, because, from then on out, we interacted as though we were together. She introduced me to her beautiful daughter one night before she dropped her off to her father's one afternoon before we went on a date. We started going out to concerts and events but mainly out of the inner city of Baltimore, due to her "separated" but not forgotten ties with her husband. I give her credit though: She tried her best to be discrete about "us" as she tried to figure out if her marriage was over. I'm not actually sure how or when her husband found out about us, or if it mentally justified his reason to actually leave her. They say there are three sides to a story—their side, your side, and the truth—and I wasn't there to see it, but the way I was told, he left her disrespectfully and embarrassingly.

He had apparently called Lisa and invited her and her girlfriends to come out one weekend to an event at a popular night club called Dreams in Washington D.C. She agreed to go and, that afternoon, she asked me if she and her older sister could come to my place to get dressed, which I didn't mind. Keeping the secret at the time, I was only informed of it being a "girls night out," but when they got to the club, they had a rude awakening. As soon as the husband saw them, he walked up with his male homeboys but also introducing his new lady friend. Lisa was so hurt and embarrassed that she forgot all about me. She didn't even call me as she would've after any other "girls night out" or the next day, which put up a red flag in my mind. The old saying is "What goes around comes around," but I never saw it coming like that, and I don't think she did either. After three days of no communicating, reality hit me and I said to myself, "What did you expect? She never belonged to you anyway. Just another experience."

That entire week I tried erasing the "bond" I thought we shared, turning the hurt into energy by hustling the streets and working part-time. I decided to put my heart back in the freezer and I used every past method to distract my emotions. Two weeks went by and, while I was outside on the block doing my side hustle, she called. I immediately hit the ignored button, but she called again immediately after. When I answered, I pretended to be having fun, joking with the fellas (immature, I know), giving her the notion that our days apart didn't faze me much. She then asked if she could come see me to explain what had been going on, and even though I was happy to hear from her, I still couldn't allow her to think her behavior was acceptable.

When I met her that night, she began to explain everything as I just stared with a blank expression. Honestly, I could see that deep hurt in her eyes as she tried hard to keep from tearing up. I felt a little sympathetic for her pain, yet I couldn't say much on the topic because, realistically, we both were wrong for our side relationship. Being a man, I don't believe in nor agree with anyone who downplays other men just to accomplish an agenda with a woman, so I wasn't going to start with her husband, even though she vented about her hate and anger towards him. After that episode, her mindset changed: She no longer wanted to be respectful of boundaries and she always wanted to go any and everywhere where familiar faces were sure to notice us. In her mind, she was getting back at her husband for humiliating her by legalizing their separation. Although I knew she was mainly motivated by hurt and a vindictive mindset, I rolled with it, because, the way I looked at it at the time, I had won. Never mind that I'd become the villain in the eyes of folks such as her sister and hate for me grew as I was now deemed a homewrecker. In my mind, I was only appreciating what someone else took for granted.

DOMINO VII

PLAYING HOUSE

Time flew by, and Lisa, her daughter, and I ended up living together. Though we were only twenty minutes away from the city, it felt far since I had spent the majority of my life living in the inner city. It was a mental challenge, being in an unfamiliar territory and moving in with a woman who already had experience of the family life, but I felt like I could earnestly call our place a home. She had found a nice size-single family house that had two levels with a huge basement that became as a second living room/office, two bathrooms, upper and lower deck in the back, a yard that measured the length of three houses that lived behind us, and a garage. There was even a nice-sized propane grill out back on the lower level. Now, at the time, if anyone would have asked me what a propane grill was, I would've looked at them as if they spoke a different language. As a matter of fact, I almost killed myself trying to impress her, stubbornly rejecting her help—I poured half a bottle of lighter fluid on the top of the grill and then lit it. All

I remember was a loud bang that blew me back about five feet up and away from where I was standing. I was undeniably embarrassed and, for a couple of seconds, I thought I was on my way to Jesus. Now, of course, Lisa had to take me to the hospital where they treated my third degree burns and looked away from what little eyelashes and eyebrows I had left.

After a month or so of trying keep off hustling in the streets, I ended up working for a rental car company where Lisa's brother was the branch manager at the time. He did me a big favor by allowing me to work there, even though all I had was a driver permit while preparing for driver school. Three years driving with no license had many folks, including Lisa, ask, how and why? Well, it's simple: When you grow up in drug-infested neighborhoods 90% of your life with a dad and uncles who are some of the most conniving people you know, you learn to mimic their ways of survival. My mother herself was a poor example, since she used to drive me daily to my elementary school in a new Audi 100 with no license—no matter, since my youngest brother's father was Baltimore drug king pin at the time. After seeing those "role models," how was I supposed to convince myself that what I was doing wrong? For the most part, I mastered the "fake it until you make it" trade, including falsifying and or embellishing on documents to get ahead in life, even though I felt it went against my nature. I tried my best to live an "honest" life, but there were just times I had to do what

I had to do to live.

Lisa and I were now in a relationship, and most of what I now know about living legit, I learned from watching her in corporate environments. She made many sacrifices, including letting me drive her car while she was at work, despite the risk of me getting pulled over and the car being impounded for my driving without a license. She helped me mentally, financially, psychologically, and emotionally, more than most woman I've encountered in my life, so for that I am grateful. For a short while, she even excommunicated herself from everyone who didn't agree with our relationship, which allowed less distractions and more time to get to know each other. I finally gave into her suggestions of a mature style of dress, going from wearing Timberland boots to Steve Maddens, baggy pants to slim-fit jeans. My first concert was with her in Washington D.C, a Mary J. Blige show featuring Wyclef John. It's funny because, when looking back at our relationship, I realize I was being schooled on things my mother or older woman in my family should've taken the time to do.

DOMINO VIII

CAN'T LOSE WHAT'S NOT YOURS

Every season must come to an end, whether from summer to spring or fall to winter. As for Lisa and I, things changed so drastically that I felt like we had skipped from summer straight to winter. It started with me getting a gut feeling that either something or someone was intruding on what we shared. On an emotional high, I thought that life had truly turned around for the better, especially looking back on how proud my grandparents were of my good changes. I was in happy land, so much that I turned off my "Get on point, stay on point" mode, which caused me to be mentally off-guard of what devilish attacks were waiting ahead.

Soon, I saw that Lisa's older sister was causing confusion between her family and I, especially their mother who was kind to me but was still influenced by the sister. She also had her so-called "friends" who threw shade because of how often Lisa and I had plans, which meant to them that I stopped her from having fun and partying. They made comments like, "Dang, girl. Even when you were with your husband, you partied with us more." Perhaps they hadn't thought about how the reason for so much freedom was to allow him to get more time for himself and his new lady. I could think of at least five other situations that pushed Lisa and I away from one another, including the fact that maybe she just got tired of pushing a young man to become a grown man in areas she was already used to being established. However, the truth of the matter was that we were both getting smacked in the face with nothing less than karma.

There was little conversation about the void between us, which ultimately enhanced my curiosity and lead to me doing things out of my character, like going through her phone. I was taught never to look too hard because even nothing can seem like something if the mind is too determined to find wrongdoing. True indeed, I found texts messages between her and another male teacher, who she explained was just a cool friend. The ironic part was that he (the teacher) was now playing my role when I first met married Lisa and now I was in the husband's shoes.

With work and the new home, I no longer had time to visit her at the school as I used to, so I didn't even notice that there was a new male teacher or that she was coming home later than usual from work. The difference of time wasn't dramatically late, but just enough to take advantage of the "lunch break" hook-up we used to share. I tried to shake it off and give her the benefit of the doubt, but after a while, I had to see for myself if there was anything serious.

One day, I decided to go to her job to be there by time she would normally be walking to her car in the parking lot. I didn't see anything out of the ordinary, just her and him walking to the car as two employees would after work. So, I called her cell phone. She answered the phone but not with her normal answer "Hey, boo," just a regular "Hey, what's up?" She then cut the conversation short by telling me she would call me back when she got in the car. She hadn't necessarily lied about what she was doing at the time, but she still didn't call me back until thirty-five extra minutes of talking to him. I looked at the guy: He had her smiling from ear to ear as I had when we first met, and he was short like me, wearing styles she dressed me in, and on top of that, he had dreadlocks similar to that of her ex-husband. Basically, if she was dating him, she was getting the best of both worlds: Me and her ex put together.

At this point, I was like Sherlock Holmes, trying to find out if I had just been the rebound to get even with or get over her husband and if she was now using this guy to get over me. That evening when she came home, I went straight to the point and asked her about the teacher guy, but she still gave me the lame Biz Markie line, saying he was just a friend. From then on, my trust in her slowly deteriorated. My mind triggered back to when the husband had asked her who I was and that same response she had give to him with a convincing voice tone. Jealous questions started popping in my head: Did he have sex with her on her lunch break too? When she met up with husband to get that under-the-table child support money, was she trying to get back together with him? Had I just found love in the wrong places? I soon saw that the way we started dating kicked off a revolving door for karma: The way you come in is the way you walk out.

DOMINO IX

LETTING GO AIN'T EASY

I remember when Lisa and I first got together officially, we agreed that we could keep our opposite sex friends. Then, shortly after that, she was a little irritated because when we were chilling together one evening, one of my friends called. We put the movie on hold, which enhanced the volume of my phone and allowed Lisa to hear another woman's voice and bits of what she was saying. Even though we only spoke briefly and no inappropriate words were exchanged, I could see that Lisa was bothered, because she made a sarcastic statement, saying, "Wow, females calling this late. She must want more than friendship." I then thought to myself, "Okay, if I have any shot at us being serious, I can't allow moments like this to cause doubt in her mind." I then changed my phone number, but not until a few days later because I didn't want her to think it was just because of a late-night call.

Since my number was changed, no other women could distractions to our relationship, and when Lisa realized what I had done, she also began ignoring phone calls from other men, except from the ex-husband and their weekly arrangement. But now, she not only began taking phone calls from male friends who all of sudden just started calling again, but also added a new male "friend" who wasn't one of the originals friends. Besides my insecure thoughts and paranoia about where she was, why she wasn't taking my calls, and why she was getting home later than normal, other factors played into the downfall of our relationship: Her bitter sister was still trying to get me out the picture, and also, a month prior this situation, Lisa had gotten an abortion. She chose to do this, not because I wanted her to, but because she was legally still married and didn't feel comfortable having a child. I believe women had the final say in these matters, so I just supported her decision as being the best thing for both of us.

But the bottom line was that I no longer wanted to tag along with Lisa and I wanted to move on with my life, since the love we had was tainted and everything we built was starting to go downhill. Constant petty arguments became our new way of conversing; it was if she was looking for a reason for us to be at each other throat. I tried staying because I did love her, but almost every time she would get off that phone, I realized someone was playing devil's advocate. Physically, I felt compelled to work things out and even lied to my peers when asked if everything was okay between her and I. Mentally, I just came to realize that it was over. There wasn't a discussion if or when we would call it quits; it just happened one day on the phone, when a harmless debate turned into a heated argument.

When I moved out, I also left the car that she co-signed for me a few months back; I didn't want to give up how much I invested in the car, but I also couldn't risk being mentally set back—I already had to deal with my lack of genuine love and abandonment issues. It took almost a year of being separated from Lisa to erase the memories, which then turned into determination fueled by hurt, bitterness, and then anger. I used it to prove to myself and everyone else who thought that I would never make it without them that I can accomplish the same or even more on my own. It's not enjoyable or healthy to be driven by anger—as my doctor says, "It's actually hurting you more than it's hurting anyone else." But regardless of what the doctor advised, I relentlessly started my journey without emotions and moved with self-motivated empowerment. While dating and chilling with new romantic interests afterwards, I had them believe I cared about them emotionally. The constant lies that created my pain were transformed into a defense mechanism that caused others to be the victims of my deeply rooted hurt. I became manipulative by using my gentleman-like manners as bait, but the truth was that I just wanted to fill the void of hurt regardless of how they felt. I didn't want emotional love, only to constantly absorb from that beginning "honeymoon stage."

DOMINO X

MY WANTS V.S MY NEEDS

After being disappointed too many times, emotions then become immune to lies that were once told before, even if the intentions meant well. I soon became exhausted of mentally abusing others because of the hurt and distrust I myself hoarded, and I started feeling lower than what I was created to be. The hyped image of who I'd become came with a heavy void of emptiness that was hidden with a smile, well-pressed clothes, shining car, and fresh cornrows. Life from the outside looking in seemed perfect, the inside I was falling apart slowly but surely and yet no one had a clue. I eventually ran into another brick wall, not being able to focus straight, which allowed me to fall right into the devil's trap: "For everything in the world-the lust of flesh, the lust of eyes, and pride of life-comes not from the Father but from the world" (1John 2;16 NIV).

They say the devil comes in many disguises: A friend, loved one, sport, TV show, food, store, or whatever your void wants and craves. One of my weakness is going after women who are challenges and intimidates the average guy. In this case, her name spoke for itself: Coca had face features that an average guy wouldn't be scared to approach, but she had that Coca Cola body shape that would tempt even a married man and made everybody thirsty. One of my close friend Stan's aunt had a "adult toys" party where I finally met her. While the fellas sat in the kitchen talking about Coca, it only gave me more motivation to go see what the hype was about. I chilled in there with my buddies Bo, Stan, and few other guys I knew for a few more minutes, but then I smoothly went into the other room where all the ladies were sitting discussing the adult toys presentation. One of my greatest attributes is being able to entertain a crowd, and what better crowd then a group of ladies? I also made it interesting by interacting with their games and giving them mature feedback on how men feel about adult bedroom situations, which instantly had the cougars curious. At the time, I was only twenty-three and they were all in their early to late thirty's. We had so much fun it made the rest of the guys come in the room too.

After the games and as everyone was preparing to leave, I got a one-on-one talk with Coca; she was interested in me but skeptical of our age difference. After noticing the reason for hesitation, I felt the need to lie about my age; I boosted it up to twenty-five, hoping to ease the thought of the gap between our age. For the first three months of our dating, everything went great and, even though she showed a few signs of being deeply spoiled, I overlooked it as nothing I couldn't handle. Being as though she had a similar background and grew up in familiar neighborhoods, I thought that maybe our upbringing instilled us with the same determined survival mindset. She was also a single mother of two, an eleven-year old son and a sixteen-year old daughter, who had manners and were respectful, automatically making me give Coca tremendous respect as a mom. Though I was still in my bachelor mode, for a second, I considered taking her a little more serious, and even knowing I loved my own space, but I entertained her offer of us sharing a place to save money. We had few clothes at each other's place since we stayed over at one another's most of the time, which may have given her the idea of moving together. If we were going to play house, why not have one?

That Valentine's day I asked my uncle to hook up my apartment. I was feeling her as a potential girlfriend (not nearly enough to even think about proposing), but regardless, the night went well and I even showed her more of my romantic side. I shared with her my past situation and, if there was a possible future for us, I recommended that we move to a new place that had neither of our history. In the meantime, I started bringing more stuff down to her place.

There were good times and there were moments of serious problems. Times when her daughter was tempted to fight two girls from the neighborhood her age and, instead of Coca going out to try defuse the situation, she jumped in the argument, threatening their entire family. I was type that tolerated little and protected my love ones by any means necessary, but the reality was that she was creating a bigger problem that could've been maturely handled. After pulling her into the house to try to calm her down and discuss solutions from our adult point of view, it still seemed as if I was negotiating with an angry teenager. From the beginning, I explained to her that, because I was on probation, I was trying to avoid ghetto drama that will create a scene and eventually get the police involved. I started to pack my belongings but, after our debate became an adult conversation and she asked me to stay, we made up.

An hour later, I had to leave for semi-pro football practice with Bo. When we returned to Coca's house, all the lights were off and I had left my car and house keys inside, expecting someone to be home. It was around 8 pm and, normally, even the kids would be home, getting ready for bed but I figured, at the most, they maybe went to the store and would be back shortly. After knocking and ringing the doorbell a few times, I decided to sit on the front steps and just wait so I wouldn't hold Bo from getting home to his family. An hour went past and my phone battery died. Then, I saw a car slowly coming down the street and something told me to turn around: When I did, I saw eyes looking from through the front door window down at me.

For a second I thought I was going crazy. As my

patience wore out, I just decided to walk to my grand-parent's a mile away, and when I got there, I called Coca's house and cell phone until she finally answered. I was frustrated but as she answered the phone so calm-ly, I tried to be as well to keep the peace, but after she explained she was inside the entire time, I instantly be-came confused and angry. I couldn't believe someone her age would do something that immature, so I ex-plained my issue with her and told her I was coming to get my stuff to really leave. I called Stan to give me a ride, and explained everything on the way there but he couldn't believe it as well; his aunt told him that Coca just recently lied that I proposed to her and we were getting married next year.

At that point, I was done. I went to knock on the door, only to hear police sirens getting closer to our loca-tion and, as I called her, she advised me to leave because they were coming for me. I was more furious about the immature game she was playing instead of simply allow-ing me to get my stuff and leave, so much so that I start-ed kicking the door until Stan got me back in the car. When the police came, I was gone, but her phone never hung up so we could hear her tell them lies that I threat-ened her and the kids. From there, the police warned me not to return there and gave her twenty-four hours to return my belongings to my apartment, and she com-plied as told. I was happy to get out of the house, but after checking the bags she dropped off, everything paused. I thought I was being punk'd by Ashton Kutcher: She cut off one of each pants leg, all my shoe string, the middle of my fitted hats, sliced the wires to my video game controllers, and never returned my name brand watches. I respect women because they are or will become mothers, but at that moment, I just wanted to give her every WWE wrestling move invented. Still, given the fact that I was on a three-year probation and because I thought about my mother and how she was in an abusive relationship, I just left it alone and took the loss.

If that wasn't enough pain, something told me to go check my closet and the nightmare wasn't over. While staying down at her house most of the time, I decided to let my youngest brother to stay at my place, and even gave him access to my back up "stash" of savings money. At the time, I knew I wasn't mature enough to give him proper time and attention but I did what was needed to keep him out of foster care. As I looked through my closets and bedroom, I noticed a few things were missing: More clothes, shoes, CDs, and movies. Automatically, first blame was going on her, but with the stash of money, I had a 357magnum pistol securely hidden, and they both were gone. I sat on the bed in disbelief and all I could think was "How can someone you love be given a chance that was never give to me and still betray me?"

Realistically, it was my fault for thinking a fifteen-year old could honestly be trusted with that much responsibility, but I thought he'd have the decency not to bite the hand that feeds him. I was outraged: My motive was betrayal, a broken heart was my ammunition, and my pride was my blindfold. That night, I went to all his friends' houses, taking back everything that belonged to me; they even told me where my brother had been hiding out. I instantly started punching him as soon as I got to him, but suddenly, images of him as a toddler flashed in my head while looking down at him on the floor: "But anyone who hates a brother or sister is in the darkness and walks around in the darkness. They do not know where they are going, because the darkness has blinded them" (1 John 2:11 NIV). As bad as I wanted to make him feel as hurt I was, I couldn't. Love somehow overpowered every emotion.

The loss of almost three thousand dollars I had stashed put me in a financial bind that forced me to liquidate my cars. My part-time job at the rental car site wasn't enough to pay my living expenses, and without a vehicle, my street mentality caused me to take the company cars after business hours. Part of me didn't approve of that decision because of how they perceived me as a top employee, but at the time, it seemed like I was thinking rationally: How else would I get to work. Still, my "halfway in, halfway out" decisions caused me to start getting sloppy about how I took the vehicles, which eventually got me caught and fired.

I could no longer afford my place so I finally let it go and moved in with my youngest aunt Jonell aka Twin and her fiancé William. I became a hermit and climbed down into a depression so deep that I literally slept on the couch for a week straight, only getting up for food. My hope in people was shattered and I questioned if there even was a God, and even if there was, I knew He didn't love me. A good friend Jarome would periodically come see me and speak uplifting verses from the Bible about God's love and mercy, which only made me even angrier at God. I was convinced and too deep in self-pity to believe that a higher power or anyone else loved me. The thought of defeat had consumed my mind, and I thought my life had to be just a bad dream and maybe "superman" just need a season of hibernation.

One day, William came home from work realizing that I been laying in the same spot since he left at five that morning. His loud frustrated voice woke me up, not to start fussing with me but, surprisingly, to approach me with genuine questions of concern that instantly caught my full attention. An inspiring lecture that I expected from my dad or an elderly family member, a Marcus Garvey mixed with Martin L. King motivational speech: "The beginning of wisdom is this: get wisdom. Though it cost all you have, get understanding. Cherish her and she will exalt you: embrace her, and she will honor you" (Proverbs 4:7-8 NIV). The grown man talk we had motivated me to join him on his store runs as we continued learning about each other. It became a normal routine and eventually we grew an unbreakable bond that allowed us both to grow and mature from each other's mistakes.

I decided to do some self-evaluating. I was puzzled

by how far I'd come and accomplished at a young age and yet having little joy. One Saturday afternoon, as I sat thinking of my new direction, my friend Drew came to visit and, as soon as I opened the door I noticed a difference in him. Both Drew and I loved to be on that grown man dress style when going to a job interview or even when fooling around trying to meet business-women downtown during lunch time. This occasion felt different: He wore that same favorite suit and his black trench coat which we always joked about, being that it always reminded me of Morris Chestnut in *Best Man* and *Shaft* all in one.

After we laughed as usual, he explained how he felt the urge to go listen to pastor Gino Jennings speak and how he reminded him of me because we both spoke straight truths that folks didn't want to hear. Part of me was on defense because my personal experience grow-ing up, preachers seemed to tell you what they wanted everyone to know (not all the truth), because it would then expose their wrong doings. But I still listened to my good friend with an open heart and he really helped me by sharing the insight of what he learned.

I was starting to understand that maybe it was true: I needed help from God to fix the void in my heart. I still didn't feel compelled to start going to church, but was inspired enough to try praying. My prayer was simple: For Him to heal my hurt with love by giving me something or someone that changes my negative reasons for living.

DOMINO XI

RESPONSIBILITY LIES WITHIN

During my time of emotion and mental recovering, I learned that the love and care that my mother was supposed to give me was a gift that could never be replaced, so it was unfair to force another woman to fill her shoes. I wasn't in a mind frame to try a relationship, but it didn't stop life from throwing propositions my way. About a month later, as I was hanging out with my cousins, I turned around to notice someone staring at me. Instantly, as we caught eye contact I realized I knew her but not sure of how; the thought of not knowing triggered my curiosity, but not enough to act on it.

That next week, my aunt called me explaining how a girl named Cameo that works with her talked about a guy throughout their work shift, and after more details, she realized it was me. I tried my best to keep my focus on my single life, but I thought what were the odds of seeing someone and being reconnected with them a few days later through a relative? Not only was I going to be introduced to that same person, but she shared with me that we graduated from the same high school. Never had I believed in coincidences, but nevertheless, it caused me to be interested enough to exchange numbers. We conversed for a while, not knowing exactly what I wanted. I just tried doing things different by keeping anything emotional to a minimum. But she couldn't hide her hurt for long: After talking on the phone, I noticed that she suffered similar abandonment issues and I immediately felt compelled to help and, if nothing more, inspire each other to overcome past hurt.

For me to keep my self-control, I needed to keep her out of sight, out of mind. But after seeing her for the second time, the conversation lasted for a few minutes but our self-control went out the window. I was conflicted in the moment because, as normal as it is for a man and woman to be intimate and my body was present, my mind was exhausted of the same formalities. I wouldn't say that I wasn't interest, just not convinced that it was supposed to be happening at that moment, or even at all. Cameo had a two-year-old son who I couldn't help but fall in love with, and there were times I would pay more attention to her son than her. Though he wasn't biologically mine, he quickly became and was treated as if he was my own junior. His father would come pick him up every other weekend, but because of the bond her son and I had, it made him begin assuming that maybe I was his real biological father. She and

I knew that it was impossible because we recently were introduced, but to him, the theory could've been right.

When he decided to completely step out of the picture, it was as if he officially passed the puck to me. I was stuck starring at her curled up on the couch crying as I sat there thinking of all the "What if's?" What if everything she said to me was a lie too? My first instinct was to get out while I could because that man could be me in the future if I stuck around, but as I walked out the door, my conscious would not allow me to keep going. A quick glimpse of my childhood flashed before me and, though my trust in her was low, I still couldn't leave knowing I could help a child break the cycle of a dysfunctional fatherless structure. I honestly wish I had a dad to tell me if my next step of action was the correct thing to do.

I stayed, but not until I had a full interrogation and making her tell the truth about everything, including her complete past life. Most people determine others' character by the mistakes they have made, but for some reason, I always saw through the chaos and valued the real person inside. Here I was trying to understand manhood while at the same time trying to lead an abandoned boy and his mother, who were just as emotionally lost as I was. Honoring my word, I did everything to create new life for us, and I even moved us into our own place, hoping that a fresh start would bring me more motivation to fully embrace them. Although I tried my best not to show it on my face, it wasn't an authentic family, playing house with a woman who didn't have my heart and raising her child as my own son.

On September 25th 2006, the mind of a boy dressed up as superman finally came face to face with its kryptonite and her name was Makenze, weighing six pounds and eight ounces. As drained as I was of life obstacles, here came a breath of fresh air that gave me a genuine reason to live and it inspired me to start a mobile carwash business. To use as a start up, I brought a small icebox truck that I would sit and stare at while imagining myself owning my company, but when I shared my idea for the truck with Cameo, she replied with laughter. I was excited that I was a new dad and grateful that we created a beautiful baby, but after three years of trying to hold onto a false hope of us being great together, I decided to move on as soon as she found employment. The apartment was in my name but I wasn't going to just leave her high and dry especially having the kids, so I moved and let her keep the place.

I hoped that being a "man" and not putting her out would at least keep me from going through the baby mama drama, but I was surely wrong. From the outside looking in and from Cameo's bitter comments about me, it could seem as though I just abandoned my responsibilities, but those who were directly around us knew that was not my character. It would've been more of an insult if I had stayed knowing there was no true connection with Cameo and that I was just there for the kids.

MEN LIE AND WOMEN LIE BUT THE TRUTH DOESN'T

I know people were doubtful about me starting my own business and I can't really blame them. I hated school and after blowing a possible football scholarship in high school, chances of going to college was slim to none. During the time being employed for any other company, the owners would be amazed at what they saw and heard of my work ethic, but I still felt underpaid and unappreciated; so I never stayed. Starting a business was never my original dream but I realized that, if I wasn't going to make that leap of faith, there was a chance that my children would experience the same that I had.

After leaving the relationship, I was now energized and focused—being the first man in the family to own a legal business would be historic—but the real mission was to continue breaking generational curses. Knowing that I could not achieve the goal alone, I decided to retrieve some help legally and spiritually. That weekend, I didn't have a desire to go out partying as a normal twenty-five-year old man would celebrate being single again; instead, I got the courage to go to God's house. I knew that God is everywhere and could see everything, but when church folks gossiped, they would say "Did you know that so and so had the nerve to do such and such…" all while in the house of God. It's funny because there are members who make it seem as if it's okay to do whatever you want, so longs as it wasn't in church. The truth is, the church cliché gave us the impression that, if we wore proper "church" attire and behaved in church, then we automatically had God's approval.

But this time, near the end of the service, the speaker said, "If there's anyone who wants to know God, walk up, give me your hand, but give God your heart." It was as if he was speaking directly to me but my feet felt like they were cemented to the floor. I was beyond nervous—my back and chest felt like they were using my heart as a drum—yet I felt God pulling me closer. My stubbornness fought extra hard to resist that desire for a better understanding of God, myself, and the knowledge to break the family curse cycle: "Ask, and it shall be given you; seek, and ye shall find; knock' and it shall be opened unto you". (Matthew 7:7). I wanted answers, but I didn't want everybody else staring at me while I walked up, like everyone could see my guilt and knew I came with drug paraphernalia and a gun outside in the car.

Still, I closed my eyes, took a deep breath and began walking towards the front of the church. My mission was bigger than negative thoughts of me. Afterwards, everyone who walked also were escorted to the new member's room. There, I met a man by the name of Earl. He had on a mailman uniform, which threw me off since that's not the "normal" appearance you would see in church, but when he started talking, his words overshadowed everything. He started off by airing all his "dirty laundry" and sharing his past life testimony about him and his woman addictions; it was if I was looking at my older self in a mirror. It was unbelievable that a person with similar past characteristic could humiliate himself just to help strangers, and I was so intrigued that, even after class, we stood in the parking lot for an hour, continuing a conversation.

I went back a few times to the class and, each time, it gave me more inspiration to do what I believed I was called to do. Courage and motivation grew rapidly within me so much that, one day, I just went down to the state office building so that I could officially legitimize the mobile carwash business I was starting. A few days later, my buddy Jay asked if I could go and show him how to do the same for the music production business he was starting. My cousin and his best friend went down with us and, as we were sitting joking and laughing while waiting for Jay's number to be called, a beautiful lady walked in the room smelling fresher than Febreze.

I tried my best not to make eye contact but I just couldn't stop peeking out the corner of my eyes. She was dressed down in cargo shorts, short sleeve shirt, sandal slippers with hair pinned up, nothing flashy or made up, but I could tell she was a woman with class the way she groomed herself. She had that Jagged Edge "Meet me at the alter" vibe. Those I came with also saw how interested I was and even encouraged me to say something to her, but as tempting as it sounded, I didn't feel the need to. After we were done and in the hallway waiting on the elevator, she too had finished her business and all I could feel was everyone eyes looking at me as if to say, "Go ahead and make your move." I introduced myself but presented it like I was only interested in promoting my company and handed her my business card, yet the quick elevator conversation showed that Shakia was interested. In a way, I kind of hoped she didn't call, not because I wasn't interested, but because I was at the point in life where I just wanted to keep focus on the new business and responsibilities as a dad. I was on the breakthrough of maturing..

That Friday, she called and immediately after we ended our greetings she blurted out, "I am probably never going to call you to get my car cleaned because my son's father already does it for me, I just wanted to let you know…" I was confused of what just happened, so I then responded, "Well, if the purpose of the call was just to inform me of that, it's very courteous but really weird." We both laughed about it and then proceeded to have an amazing, mature conversation. After almost an hour of us on the phone, the energy between us must have been so powerful that we started thinking of ways to finish our conversation in person. When we met up, we talked and joked, which made her more comfortable to share how she grew up in a similar background, was divorced, and had three kids. It inspired me that she was only about six years older than me and had a business, owned a three-bed room house, drove a Ford Expedition truck, and a Mercedes CLS 550. Although I applauded her for her achievements, I was more impressed with how she wasn't defeated by society's statistic prediction growing up in an environment that I too came from.

We also shared that mindset of respecting reality but sometimes taking a moment to put adult life on pause to enjoy life like two little kids in the playground. Running errands together at department stores such as Ikea would turn into nonstop laughing adventures for three, four hours. No matter how either of our days had been up until that point, once we spoke on the phone or in person, the moment would be overshadowed by smiles. Just as any other relationship starts, there were no complaints and never questions about whereabouts or who was hanging around. Things were good as time went on but my focus on getting the business booming helped me to stabilize and steady my feelings towards her. I thought about starting a family eventually, but was no longer driven by this urge and I was cool with us just interacting as friends, seeing each other or talking when we both had time to. Both of us being business owners, I tried to not bother her during business hours, which I thought would be a "turn on," yet her negative assumptions made me more "turned off." Before things could go south, I decided to give her a little more access to my life to help her gain a better understanding of my mindset. There wasn't any room left for her to make assumptions because, when we weren't together, we were on the phone.

Though we shared a lot of time together I wasn't naïve and certainly discerned an anchor (male presence) that kept her from consistently fighting for the level of commitment she really wanted with me. I mean yes, we verbally said that we were both single, but both of our actions gave clue that time was still given elsewhere. Some won't admit it, but realistically, there's a ninety percent chance that, when you first meet someone, before you take your throne as king/queen, someone else was keeping the seat warm, whether for intimacy or just filling a void. Already understanding that, I didn't make a fuss about it simply because there was no guarantee of us becoming more serious than the benefited "friendship" we had. Shakia wanted me, who stole her heart, but her ex still had her mind because they had a history.

She started introducing me to close relatives and people who were important to her, but at times, I would see her watching everyone's reaction towards me. It's normal to hope that important people in your life would accept your lover, but I felt more like I was in court trial than in a room with friends. Her folks were cool, but it just seemed as though everyone was in a competition with each other or had to get praise from everyone for their accomplishments. Shakia wasn't a bourgeois person but some would say that she seemed stuck between personalities: At times, she displayed this trustworthy, loving person who simply wanted to be accepted as a fun, inspiring, God-fearing woman just waiting for her soul mate. On the other hand, mainly during the late evenings, she became a money-hungry, "do what I want," single diva who had a gambling addiction and craved attention. Not sure of who I was possibly going to be involved with didn't help my trust: It was like being involved with Halle Berry half the time and while the other half was more like Cat Woman mixed with Foxy Brown Cleopatra. Then again, who am I to talk when I was keeping up an image of Super Fly who lived more secretly than James Bond 007. Maybe that why I was so intrigued in her: She was nothing more than a mirror reflection of me. Whether I liked it or not I was learning that I was only attracting what I had become, even if it wasn't exactly what I wanted; thus, if I wanted better, I had to become greater than what I myself was.

Becoming more serious meant we had to start at a middle ground where we could create a "clean slate." We decided to start attending church, not knowing that the church she went to was the exact one I used to visit as a teenager with elder cousin Maree and her sons, cousins Jarrod and Terrell, only because it was like a woman heaven for us. As an adult, it was a different experience; No, I didn't start to shouting or dancing, but it was like an epiphany or feeling that gave me comfort that I was heading in the right direction. I was fully confident that she was the one who God sent for me, so without hesitation, I did what I could to give her mental comfort and even fell in the roll as dad figure for the kids. My daughter was my main priority but I made sure I attended all her kids' events from sports and school achievements to her daughter's baptism. I supported them not to "win" Shakia over, nor to compete with their biological dads, but because of how her kids embraced me as their authority figure. Our future looked bright, and going to church grew us more spiritually than physically, but I could feel a dark force pulling her away from me when her cousin and friend clouded her vision. Genesis 1:4 says "God saw that the light was good, and he separated the light from darkness."

On her daughter's eighteenth birthday, I came by the house to sing happy birthday, but because Shakia and I had a disagreement about her ex-boyfriend earlier that day, things didn't feel right. Afterwards, I decided I had to leave to not ruin the party since her mom and I weren't on the same page, but I also felt unexplainable bad vibes. At first, I thought it was probably just me, but when I saw the look on Shakia face after she declined a certain phone call, I had an idea of the problem. As I was leaving Shakia was trying to convince me to stay in her house, but that intuition urged me to leave and not wait another minute. As soon as I put the key in the ignition, it's like I could feel a negative force behind me; being from the streets, I normally would check my surroundings but I was distracted by Shakia begging me to stay.

In that instance, she walked pass my car towards an SUV that was parked a few cars down behind me. I was confused until I saw a guy get out and started fussing at her. Immediately, the protection instinct kicked in so I quickly drove towards them, but as I got closer, another instinct kicked in: Wisdom. It was like God paused time for me to evaluate the scenario, realizing there was no need to jump and protect her because he wasn't there to do harm to her—just a drunk, jealous dude being immature. When I first started coming over to her house, one of first things Shakia made clear was that, though her ex-boyfriend had stayed at her place a couple of times while they were together, she assured me that him nor anyone else would ever do a "pop up" visit. But here we were in that exact debacle.

Intelligent as that decision was for me to leave, my anger wanted me to hurt him severely for even posing a threat to my life. I also felt betrayed that she didn't even have the decency to warn me about the danger, instead of making it seem as if she wanted me to stay. Playing the devil's advocate only blew up back in her face, not only making her look bad but also allowing her to lose what we were growing to become. The truth of the matter is, regardless of if I would have stayed and we fought for her, whether physically or just verbally, it still wouldn't have given her clarity of who was right for her because she had no true clarity of what was right or wrong about herself.

DOMINIO XIII

THE ILLUSIONS OF HAPPINESS

As time went on and throughout the passing years, I tried staying focused on the journey of growth. Yes, I made many mistakes along the way, including getting into some legal trouble, but nothing stopped me. I was wiser than and the maturity of manhood challenged me to right my wrongs and fight to not repeat them. By this time in my life, to split apart from Shakia wasn't impossible to cope with. I was truly disappointed but, then again, I saw it coming. My feelings just leaped towards false hope.

I decided to recuperate by continuing church services while making sense of my life and God's role and love in my life. I was in my mid-twenties and still trying figure out manhood and fatherhood with little guidance, but resilience kept me pushing forward, searching for answers of my purpose: "Therefor repent and turn back, so that your sins be wiped out, that the season of refreshing may come from the Lord" (Acts 3:19 NIV).

The seasons were changing and winter was here. I

just purchased a new apartment for Makenze and my-self, and to earn a steady income, William helped me get a part-time job at Mercy Medical Hospital in down-town Baltimore City. Within sixty days of working there, I received a raise and then was promoted with a new position by the vice president of the department. Between being blessed with a new place that gave me more quality time with my daughter, my new job pro-motion, a side business, and going to church, I felt in-vincible and nobody could tell me different. I thought I was given the best of both worlds now: Living the ultimate bachelor life, dating multiple females with no strings attached, partying on Saturday's, and church on Sunday's.

Believing that my new way of living was okay with God, I began feeling myself. Pride was my successor and Mr. Untouchable was my alter ego. I thought that God was gifting me with blessings, but I forgot that the devil give gifts too and uses them to trap us all. I was well-known throughout my life but my hood fame went to a higher status of superstar inside this bar lounge I started going to. I drank more liquor and wine there then in my twenty odd years of living. At first, it started out with casual hang outs on Saturdays, but that soon became Friday, Saturday, and even some Sundays, right after church service.

Then, one Friday night, every sign said not to go there that night, but I didn't take heed of the warnings. Jesus himself could've stood at the door and said don't go inside this place, but it would've went into one ear and out the other. I received three phone calls of close people trying to talk me out of not leaving the house that night, but it just seemed as if folks were trying stop me from having fun. One call came from a good friend who was head security there, who explained, "Little bro, the spot is half empty, DJ sucks, and there are barely any women here." He was baffled when it didn't stop me, but in my mind it was Friday night and I was going to get in free anyway. Plus, I could kill some time before until my lady friend got out of her party.

The lounge let out at 1:45am and I arrived at 1:20am. Normally, I would've grabbed a bottle of wine and left back out, but for some odd reason, the lounge got flooded with more people. With the music pumping, the dance floor crowded, and beautiful ladies offering to buy me drinks, I was the man, a shorter, light-skin version of Denzel. Boredom and loneliness at home got the best of me and the devil used my addiction to the fame and false love as a trap for my destruction. I heard a soft voice in my head urging me to leave, but I was convinced everything was cool. But all that spotlight fueled a drunk stranger with envy and he began antagonizing everyone sitting with me; his words made it clear that I was the target. A fight would inevitably ensue.

The night ended tragically, totally the opposite of what any of us expected: A man half dead and me being the prime suspect wanted for attempted murder.

DOMINO XIV

DEFINING LOVE

I was arrested three days later after the incident occurred. My silence and non-cooperation put the states attorney and judge in a position to deny me of a pre-release bail three different times. In a blink of an eye, my life went from walking on cloud nine to twenty-three hour lockdown with only one hour of recreation time. I didn't understand; I was minding my business just simply having fun. After all, church folks say, "It's okay to enjoy yourself, as long as you ain't hurting nobody."

My ex-girlfriend Ebony and Bro Earl from church were the first ones to come visit me and I expected the "I told you so" speech, but instead, Earl spoke in an unfamiliar charismatic way. He shared with me that God isn't trying to stop us from having fun—earth was designed to enjoy. However, Satan will try to use good for bad purposes. He explained how one of Jesus' first miracles was at a wedding reception party; when the wine ran out, Jesus gave a sign of His glory by turning water into wine. Earl even confessed how he used to party the same as I did, but God showed him that going dancing wasn't God's issue, but instead the dark environment it took place in: "Do not be yoked together with unbelievers. For what do righteousness and wickedness have in common? Or what fellowship can light have with darkness" (2 Corinthians 6:14).

During my time being incarcerated, I learned that I was looking for love in all the wrong places: Sex, woman, jobs, money, material things, parties, relationships etc. There was no joy. The moment that was the straw that broke the camel's back was when the mother of my child brought my daughter to visit me: Seeing the distraught look in my daughter's eyes and face wet with tears made me feel like my heart was being ripped out my chest. I stood strong in the visiting room to give her comfort but when I returned to my cell, twenty plus years of bottled up tears poured down my face. I was face to face with reality: The hurting pain of abandonment that I felt as a kid was being transferred by me onto my own child.

While on my knees, God allowed me to remember all the women I hurt unknowingly and with bad intentions. I was repeating the generational curse on them because I didn't break the cycle. I couldn't imagine twenty years of my daughter growing up without me and calling someone else her dad or dating wrong types of guys because I wasn't there to be the example of a real man. With very few financial supporters and my lawyer fees piling to ten thousand plus dollars, in addition to not being able to get out on bail, my hands were tied.

A few good buddies of mine inside were having a Bible study and invited me to come check it out. The slight bitterness of my situation caused me to be hesitate but playing dominos wasn't going to help me either. After hearing life testimonies and knowing that most of them were receiving ten to twenty years, I couldn't believe how calm they were, just by having faith in God. These "dangerous" convicted felons focused not so much on physical freedom, but instead on spiritual freedom. Bro Blackwell, a seventy-five-year old pastor came every Wednesday and had a way of leading the studies that wasn't being taught like in church on the outside. By being a drug dealer and street runner himself back in the day, he could relate to us; however. he didn't sugarcoat anything for anybody. Straight truth was what he spoke and sung praise songs with a smile.

I was never the type to just hear and believe anything someone says, regardless of how good it sounded. But one morning around three o'clock something told me to write down all the names of the women I dated. I laughed to myself at first because it had been so long ago that I didn't know where to start, but as I began to write the names down, the full memory of them came to me as clear as day. The more names I wrote, the clearer I understood how I hurt them, but in ways I didn't realize. Then, that something said to me, "How would you feel if these things too happened to your daughter?" I filled up five pages of a writing pad and immediately asked for forgiveness—I was certain that I didn't want Makenze to receive that hurting karma.

Exhausted of stressing and figuring out things alone, I challenged God: If He was real and the teachings in the scriptures were true, then I would give my all to do His way. My only request in return was to win at trial so I could get another chance to raise my daughter and break my family generational curse: "But God is faithful and fair. If we admit that we have sinned, He will forgive us our sins. He will forgive every wrong thing we have done. He will make us pure" (1 John 1:9). My brothers in Christ, Ron, Kendrick, Rodje, and I were now rebels with a positive cause, not having to convince anyone of God's peace; instead, our actions were examples of our commitment, which won other inmates to Christ.

The peace eventually impacted our entire tier. For many years the section 3D was always known as the rowdiest and most dangerous in the whole prison, but soon, we became the calm tier with the least violence. Within two to three months later, it went from four to sixteen of us including those charged with murder, theft, drug charges and even gang members who all wanted the same change. It was an accomplishment never heard of before then, so much so that the prison sergeant and lieutenant came personally to investigate.

Around the same time, my previous coworker Darlene came to offer her assistance by making calls and visits to those I needed to reach. A couple days later, I was placed in a line up, so that a witness could identify me as the suspect, but I couldn't be pointed out. Three weeks before retrial, my close friend from high school Rashid came to visit and said God put it on his heart to help with my lawyer fees. That same week my cousin Lamika flew from California to help as well. They both were the last two I expected to come, so I truly believed they were sent from God. The day before court, my lawyer came to visit me after not seeing me for months. He began reiterating that my balance was not fully paid but, because he believed if I returned home he would be paid, he was still going to represent me. The next morning before court, I called before school to tell my daughter that I loved her, and her mother told me that last night she dreamed that God told me to read Jeremiah 39:11: "'For I know the plans I have for you,' declares the Lord, 'plans to prosper you and not harm you, plans to give you hope and a future.'" I had faith, not just in things going well for me, but in the fact that, for the first time in my life, I didn't run away from commitment. It was now God's turn to see if He would honor my challenge. Right before our case was called, there were a few other offers presented by the prosecutor, but with confidence, I rejected them all because none of them benefited my cousin (Xavier). Not being pointed out in the line up played a key role on my behalf, but still an eye witness was going to testify against my cousin; he only had a public defender, so it didn't look good for him. Soon, my lawyer made me aware that, after talking to the prosecutor, they had lack of evidence against me. During a short recess, a deal was made to my lawyer: If I pled guilty, I would finish five more months on home detention and three-year supervised probation, and my cousin would then receive seven years instead of twenty. The catch was that we both had to agree upon the deal; being unable to communicate with one another, we just allowed our loyalty and love to decide. My cousin was willing to except the time and so I could be completely free, but at the same time I wasn't going to allow them to throw him under the bus with jail time.

The judge seemed like he wanted a guilty conviction as bad as the family and mainly after the prosecutor painted us as "monsters," because the doctors had to freeze part of the brain to save the victim. Eventually, I recognize that I was guilty of playing a part in our case, so I decided to accept the plea offer; my cousin and I had made eye contact and agreed on it. It was done, and after the case, both my lawyer and the prosecutor came back to my holding cell. They expressed that it had been a long time since they witnessed a serious case such as ours start and end with loyalty and love that never wavered.

God did it! He honored my challenge when I decided to first challenge myself and display my loyalty and honor for Him: "Therefore the Lord, the God of Israel declares:' I promise that members of your family would minister before me forever. 'But now the Lord declares: Far be it from me! Those who honor me I will honor, but those who despise me will be disdained" (1 Samuel 2 NIV)

DOMINIO XV

BREAKING THE CURSE

President Barack Obama said, "Change will never come if we wait for some other person or some other time. We are the ones we've been waiting for. We are the change that we seek." I was released three days after court and was now able to start the journey of rebuilding. However, I knew I had to be strategic about it since I was still on home detention. It was normal to be thrown a big party when getting out of jail, but as for me, I wanted to continue being in the "out of sight, out of mind" thought, and just wanted quiet and a real meal. My friend Paul and his wife Jan allowed me to stay with them and welcomed me in with a home-cooked meal. Regardless of circumstances or our time apart, Paul and I always kept an "open door" policy for each other when in need.

Throughout the week, I kept Makenze with me when her mother went to work and, at times, I would just stare at her, mentally apologizing for allowing ignorance to separate us. I was so excited that I was home in time for her fifth birthday, and Paul and Jan helped to give her a surprise party. Her smile brought me so much joy that we turned the party into a pajama party sleepover, and the next day, Paul and I had one of the biggest water battles against the kids. I knew I had to live up to be the hero she saw me as and build her daily with the same genuine love and joy that I never got from who I looked at as a hero.

The least people that knew I was home from jail, the less I would become distracted, so I did my best to stay under the radar. After three months without drama, financial issues, and sex, I knew that one of them, if not all would tempt me and throw me backwards. Finding employment and a future wife were the first two things on my agenda that I knew would keep me focus and be the foundation for breaking the family curse. But I was running into the opposite, constantly being denied of employment and even getting the job on the spot three different times until they checked my criminal background. The rejections became overwhelming and, sure enough, the devil used old "street" buddies, offering me $30,000 dollars to make a simple phone call. It was easy money and the thought of me not being able to financially take care of my daughter had me feeling desperate. But I also wasn't desperate enough to allow another chance of being separated from her. All I could do was fall to my knees and see if God had an answer to my financial dilemma.

In the middle of praying, a thought came to me that

I should call unemployment and social services. I was eligible for unemployment from the time on my last job at the hospital and social services qualified me for $150 dollars in food stamps. I was amazed that He answered my prayers again. The financial part was handled for now, so the enemy's new target was my hormones that were craving an appetite in my abstinence. They say that "where the mind goes, the man will follow" and the only thing my mind was thinking about was certain women from the past, so I called a few. Then I made a discovery: The conversations always started out well but the women became disinterested when they realized that the man I had become was less "interesting" than the popular boy I had been. The fact that I held an intellectual conversation for days without using profanity or entertaining any of my past negative urges, almost rendered our phone calls irrelevant. I explained to them about my new lifestyle and how God felt about my old behaviors, they all said, "We're only human and nobody's perfect."

I don't blame them: I was once a victim of that statement and it made me feel better about all the dirt I did; but then, I realized that is was all just an excused to justify wrongdoings. God read my mind and knew that I was going to come out to use that excuse again, so He lead me to truth on what was written about by being "perfect." The Greek word *telos*, which is translated as "perfect," can equally be translated into "goal, end, or purpose." The *telos* of a thing is that point to which a thing yearns to be, the purpose for which a thing was built: "Be perfect, therefore, as your heavenly Father is perfect" (Matthew 5:48). It does not imply that perfection has been attained, but it is the trajectory towards which the essence of a thing strives, basically meaning growth or maturing. In my past lifestyle, I had been perfect as a whoremonger and street hustler, and praised for it by my so-called "friends" and "loved ones." But now, I'm genuinely trying to become perfect at letting Jesus take the wheel. No matter how anyone felt about my new outlook on life, my new change was a great improvement that also secured my child's future.

Finally, a car deal with only two months of employment, a used car dealership approved me for a vehicle, even though I had extremely bad credit and had no money to put down. The more I grew mentally, the better results came back to me physically and financially. But, for the moment. there wasn't an answer for my emotionally needs. People always assumed that I desired a lot of women and there was a time where no one ever would've believe that I was going to be settle down with just one. The funny thing is that I used to hear it so much that I convinced myself that I wasn't going to either, while knowing that I honestly desired the exact opposite.

Within my time away, I not only did some soul-searching but also a self-evaluation of my behavior and commitment issues towards women. The first thing I realized is that, in my heart, I did want to just settle down, but because of the abandonment issues I suffered from my mother constantly leaving me, I built a wall of distrust for all women. The next step after admitting I had that problem was to forgive my mother, so that bitterness could no longer hold me captive, and I could then try to appreciate women better. With an improve mindset, it was still hard to choose the right partner for me. Whenever I came home from work, I tried to go straight in the house to help me resist the many temptations outside. A man living right is still just a man, and the warm weather brought out everything except fully-dressed women. The club scene was negative, going back to ex-girlfriends wasn't moving forward, and others I was introduced to were cool and some really pretty, but just not settling down material.

I then decided to try out this website that a buddy of mine used before and that he said he met a good woman through. At first, I was reluctant because it kind of made me feel like I was desperate, but the reality was, what I was trying wasn't working and, worst case scenario, I could always go back to square one. It was started out as a weird but fun experience, yet I was still skeptical while looking through the profiles pictures and bios. I found a few prospects but they were more beauty than brains. After three days on the website, I decided to close the account and go back meeting women the old fashioned way, but right before closing out, I was mentally grabbed by a beautiful smile. I didn't know her and I had never talked to her, but instantly her smile began conversing with my smile. To top it off, there were key words that peeked my interest even more such as how she put God first and her definition of a "girl's night out" was them eating sushi and having a glass of wine. When I messaged her, I was soon hooked by her consistent intellectual conversations: "Charm is deceptive and beauty is fleeting; but a woman who fear the Lord is to be praised" (Proverbs 31:30).

Her name was Kristin, a single mother of a two-year old. She was six years younger than I was, which would normally be a turn off, but she had this "Give me a chance and I'll prove it" demeanor that overshadowed her age. Knowing her child was recently conceived had me cautious until I learned the details of her baby daddy situation, and the reason for them separating. I quickly understood that, if Kristin and I were going to be together, it was obvious I was going to be that fill in father figure for her daughter Audriana. Kristin had a great support system from family and close friends, which helped manage the responsibility as a young mother but still gave her time to herself.

Kristin and I were the total opposite of each other. She grew up in a church-based family environment that had minor issues and tried their best to show the children structure. Though their family wasn't financially wealthy, the unity between them passed down from the elders onto the children was what gave them a rich spirit, which gave Kristin motivation to be an A student. As a single mom from the inner city, her mother pushed for any financial aid she could find so that Kristin wouldn't have to go to any public elementary and middle schools. She was sheltered throughout her youth, so much so that, once she went to a public high school, her eyes began to fascinated by all the things she was deprived from seeing or even hearing about.

Kristin was considered a "nerd" because she was one of the top students in high school, and the pressure of feeling like an outcast weighed heavy on her. She worked a part-time job while in high school up through college, which then allowed her to afford clothes, and accessories that gave her more of an "in-crowd" appearance. In college, though still exceptionally smart in school, her new appearance began attracting the opposite of what she was raised for. Her father not being in her life didn't help the situation, since she was green to recognizing wolves in sheep's clothing.

Her second year in college, she found herself falling into bad habits and in an unhealthy relationship that she was planning to leave, but not before discovering that she was pregnant. She was raised to not believe in abortions, so after realizing she was in it alone, she quickly moved back home and stayed with her aunt and uncle while preparing for the baby. When Audriana was born, Kristin became a full-time mom, and only being in her early twenties, her social life was put on pause. When she felt the urge to start dating, she gave that same dating website a chance.

Since we met, she never skipped a beat on showing me how serious she was and used to drive all the way to where I lived just to bring me breakfast at least three times a week before I went to work. As great as she was to me, I still had second guesses about us getting any closer. I gave God my word that, if He would allow me to meet someone who was beautiful mentally and spiritually, then I would consider getting married. It's like I was always meeting attractive women, but no one who could hold my attention like Kristin. I decided to give more focus on her and find out what was it that had me so curious about her.

DOMINO XVI

LOVE DOESN'T GIVE UP

A year had gone by and everything was going great between us but my uncertainty of taking it a step further had become our road block for us, and soon enough, a storm came that was going to either make or break us. My roommate broke the news to me that he had lost his job and couldn't afford to pay the rent, and because I was just getting on my "feet," I knew I couldn't do it alone. I felt frustration: Right when I thought things were going forward, the enemy was trying to pull me backwards.

As the moving day was getting closer, the thought of trying to stay with someone who respected what I had with her was getting pushed further and further out my mind. It was crunch time and the feelings we had for each other wasn't going to provide shelter over my head. I told my friend Paul about it and he said to come back there (he too was separated from). Kristin came to visit and cook meals for us every other day and everything was smooth; but not too long after, things went bad again. The contract agreement between Paul and his landlord didn't go as well as Paul planned, which gave us both a deadline to move out by, and after moving from there, I moved several more times. Each time, Kristin gave me support. My frustration was at an all-time high, especially after my job started cutting down on overtime hours and my manager and I started bumping heads to the point of almost getting physical. I not only needed a job to provide for my child, but also because probation required that I remain employed.

One day though, I walked off and got in my car. Kristin talked to me and convinced me to not quit; she even asked if we could pray together and suggested that I should let God lead my final decision. I ended up not quitting the job, but I knew I needed more income so I started working part-time for the *Baltimore Sun*, delivering papers overnight. It was a humbling experience, and I felt like I was back in the 1970's, only instead of carrying a bag over the shoulders while riding a bicycle, I had a car, packed with over two hundred plus newspapers. Sometimes between jobs, I only had enough time to take a two or three hour nap because of how far the jobs were from each other, which gave me minimum time with Kristin or my daughter.

One Friday, as I was going on the Eastside of town to help William, I was pulled over and arrested, being charged with crimes I had no prior knowledge of. While inside, there was a guy who was arrested for running around downtown while fully naked after some "friends" put drugs in him while at a party. Everyone disrespected and made funny jokes about his charges, but God put it in my heart to talk to him and help him understand that the ignorance he was surrounded by allowed him to be in his situation. After our conversation, he was confident in giving God a try: "Do not forget to show hospitality to strangers, for by so doing some people have shown hospitality to angels without knowing it" (Hebrews 13:2 NIV).

Sunday morning came, I finally was released on bail, and so I walked a few blocks to the nearest place where I could use a phone. At first, a part of me felt relieved to be out of there, but the other half was a little disappointed nobody was outside waiting. But then again, I remembered this process was unpredictable. I called William and he told me that Kristin was in church, but he then gave me a lecture on why he believes she was the one for me. He explained how she constantly called the jail commissioner to find out if I was granted a bail, then, in the middle of the night, went down to pay the bail and stayed awake, waiting for them to assure her that the bail had been posted. At that moment, it was as if all doubt about me giving her my all was erased and I didn't need any further confirmation about making a real commitment. Any woman who would stick by me when my stability was constantly crumbling, show me consistency by proving her desire to be with me in ways seen and unseen, and still have the strength to go to our heavenly Father's throne on my behalf is worth marrying.

The next week, after work one day, I just felt it was time to look for a ring. I knew if I didn't do it that day, the enemy would convince me of reasons why I shouldn't. William and I went from store to store, trying to find a ring and I eventually found one that was perfect for Kristin. William's face was filled with joy as a father's would be, sending his son off to college.

I met Kristin at the train station where she leaves the car and rides the train to work. When she arrived, William walked to her and explained how something was wrong with the car tire. When came around to the other side of car, I was already on one knee, proposing to her. The funniest part was, because she would get off work just in time for the last midnight train, her facial expression at first was between concerned, happy, and sleepy all at once. I was determined to break the curse of lies that always had me feeling that the next level of life wasn't where I belonged.

We set a date for the wedding and a date to move into our new apartment. We decided to do things old fashioned way and not move in together until we were officially married. We also made a vow before God that we wanted Him to honor us and so we wanted honor Him by not having any sexual intercourse until our wedding night. Of course, not even two day later I was regretful, but even after almost giving in a few times, we managed to keep our word. Two weeks before the wedding, we signed our lease for our new apartment and, for safe measures, we decided that she still stay with her aunt to guarantee our agreement. I never was the type who enjoyed strip clubs even in my past lifestyle, so for my bachelor party, the fellas and I went to DC to a lounge so I could get my last "single man" boogie on. We had an awesome time out, but the next day, I over-slept and didn't even hear Bo (my best man) calling, knocking, or banging on the door for almost an hour.

The groomsmen and I finally made it to the church where the wedding was held, and waited in the back as the guest arrived. While we were waiting, Reece start-ed free-styling a hilarious song he made up and then he mentioned the word "ring," and I instantly remem-bered I left the ring home. Reece and Bo drove as fast they could to get the ring and, by time they made it back to the church was our exact cue to walk into the sanctuary: "He who finds a wife finds what is good and receives favor from the Lord" (Proverbs 18:22 NIV).

The wedding was amazing and any doubt in my mind before as now dominated by that miraculous beauty of pure love that walked down that isle and be-came one with me. The years that Kristin and I have been married has been an inspirational blueprint of Hope that several others have used to welcome love and matrimony into their own lives. In July of 2016, my business partner Chris and I started another mobile cleaning business called New Visionz L.L.C, that was inspired by my eyes being clear of the new vision for our future. We have been gifted with three commer-cial contracts and a month after our grand opening on

August 30th, God blessed Kristin and I by allowing us to buy our first house.

From my childhood, I have been living with deep-rooted hurt from the constant lies that were embedded in me by loved ones and situations. For many years that same hurt is what I used to deteriorate others who gave me their hope and, though my heart wanted to trust love, I was imprisoned by anger and vindictiveness. The road I was on only lead me to dead ends, but when I decided to allow God to lead me, the path only produced success.

STOP LYING TO YOURSELF

After reading my story, you now see how lies told by love ones and yourself can grow deep roots. Sometimes, they grow so deep within you that it becomes a characteristic or even puts you in situations that could've been prevented. Here are some possible scenarios and how daily lies can affect you and others.

HEARING

Have you ever rushed to get to that appointment or personal event, knowing you should have got your outfit together the night before but you had figured, "Nope, I'm good. I'll have enough time"? Imagine this scenario: That morning, you think for sure that you set your alarm as you normally do, and since the weather had been awesome all week, you don't watch the next day's forecast that predicts a thunderstorm starting at midnight and moving into the early mornings. So, in the middle of the night, the storm knocks your power out for few hours while you are asleep, including your clocks, and your phone completely dies.

The next morning comes and you inner voice says "Get up!" So now, you jump up and it's 8:30 am, but really had to be up 7:15am at the latest, because it's urgent that you be there on time at 9:30 am and you live 35 minutes away. So you are now stuck with either a quick birdbath at the sink or just go hard and wash your underarms and personal areas because there is no way you have time to fully bathe. Normally, bathing is a must for you before leaving the house, but you tell yourself "I'll just fully bathe as soon as I get back." You rush out the house, and while in the car, you try to eat that slice of toast while also brushing your hair in the mirror at every stop light. You are convinced that the expressway will be faster by 9:15 am, but, once you're on, you realize that traffic is at a complete stop from an accident and the emergency responders are just pulling up to the scene. Now you're going to be super late or miss that appointment that took two months to schedule. Maybe it was your company's regional presentation that you prepared for three weeks and would have set you up for that promotion, or maybe it was your child's honor roll ceremony.

People old or young wonder if the voice they hear inside themselves is something they should actually listen to or not; regardless, we all have said numerous of times "something told me to do so." The truth is, there are three voices that we hear: Yourself, God, and demons. With or without daily scriptures, it's a mess trying figure out which voice is who and when to listen to it. For the most part, as you mature by learning from bad decisions and not following the right voice, you start to learn the difference. When us humans think about a decision, it's based upon our emotions and how we feel about doing something. When God speaks, it's more of what's best for us, regardless of our feelings at that moment. A demon's voices and our own are very similar, because that demon is trying convince you to do something that revolves around your fleshly desires. Demons often disguise their voices, speaking in the first person, "I" instead of "you," making it seem as if they are speaking for you. For example, the thought "I am a loser," because it comes to you in a first person, you assume you thought it yourself. Even if the thought wasn't yours, once you believe you thought it, the effects are just as damaging. It now starts a negative ripple effect within your life psychologically, physically, and or financially, simply following what we heard from that wrong voice.

SMELLING

Imagine another scenario: Before leaving home for work, you walk past the kitchen, only to catch a whiff of a foul odor, which you think to yourself, "That trash smells horrible." So you walk towards the trashcan to realize that, that isn't where the smell is coming from, so you start to follow your nose and you find out that it's the meat you took out of the refrigerator yesterday morning to thaw out to cook last night.

Other things were on your mind so, when you came home last night, you went straight to bed. At this point, you realize how bad the smell is, but immediately look down and say to yourself, "I can just take the trash out as soon as I get home, because I don't want my work clothes smelling like this stink." You then put the smelly meat inside of a little grocery bag, tie in a knot, and then put it inside the trashcan closing that up tight as well. Yes, the smell is still lingering a little but it makes you feel better that it no longer smells as bad.

You then go to work, have a great day, so good that you invite a couple of your co-workers over to the house. You even told them that you were going to throw together a quick meal. Of course, they take you up on your offer. You finally get to your house, not realizing that you never took that smelly meat outside to the dumpster. Then, you open the front door and the horrible smell from the morning has tripled, because you never even opened a window. Your house is now an embarrassment. Guess who is now going to be the talk of the company?

This scenario may not relate to you because maybe the type of person you are would've just taken the trash out, but how many of us have been embarrassed from not resolving another odor issue? How about a time when you forgot to apply deodorant and you are soon find yourself in a crowd? A time when you agreed to give someone a ride, but weren't thinking about the spilled food from days before that you left to clean up "another time?" I am sure there are plenty scenarios coming to mind now, but my point is that, if you simply deal with what you smell when you smell it, procrastination won't come back to haunt you.

TASTE

Last Thanksgiving, you decided to go over to your soon-to-be spouse's grandmother's house because you really want to get to know the family better. The whole family was cool and showing you a lot of love, and as far as the grandma goes, she's the sweetest lady you ever met. So sweet that she is the first person to acknowledge you as family even before the wedding day. On top, everybody was bragging about that one famous yam dish grandma makes for every family gathering.

Dinnertime arrived, and the food looked and smelled good—everything packed on your plate, especially grandma's yams. You started digging in: The turkey tasted moist, the macaroni and cheese were good, the stuffing, cranberry sauce, and even the sauerkraut (which you normally don't like) were all banging. So you said to yourself, "If all this tastes fabulous, the yams are going to be the best ever!" Before you start off eating anything you would normally take a sample bite first, but since you were so into all the other courses, you then proceeded to stuff your mouth with a whole fork full of yams.

While everybody stared at you with confidence, you struggled to hold your composure. The yams tasted as if grandma had poured a half-pound of the cinnamon factory on them and your nose hairs burned. In fact, they tasted like pieces of oak wood, and you got stuck trying to not let tears come down your face from the taste of cinnamania.

So this year, you take your best friend to this Thanksgiving gathering to show them how cool your spouse's family is. The food comes out and everybody begin grubbing and you don't have as much yams on your plate, because you remember "that taste." You are also convinced that maybe grandma just over did herself with the cinnamon last time or maybe she nodded off in the rocking chair and the bottle dumped completely over. Either way you had to try it again for respect's sake, but just not as much as you did last time. What you didn't remember was that you forgot to warn your best friend of the possible mishap, but you still can't because you are at the table now. You convince yourself, "Maybe it won't be a bad experience for them," even though you know exactly how it tastes. After taking a bite, your best friend starts to cough badly with his eyes watering up, the same symptoms you had after eating grandma's yams. But all you can do is sit with that lying look of confusion. Now the whole table is looking at you because, after all, it's your guest that you invited to their family dinner.

Do we have the power to know what something is going to taste like before we eat it? No, and even when we smell it first, it's still impossible to know exactly how would taste. But once you taste something, you must be truthful about how you feel and also remember those associations. Things in life always go better the next time if you are truthful of what wasn't good and stick with what you know for sure. Be honest with loved ones who trust in you, or at least warn them about unpleasant situations that not even you want to deal with.

FEEL

There was a time that you were introduced to an area of life that your curiosity craved for, even before you were properly introduced to it, whether "it" was gambling, smoking cigarettes/marijuana, drugs, alcohol, driving without a license, sex with a married man or woman, etc. All of those examples that you, including myself, have done, tried doing, or thought about doing are all situations that were supposed to make you "feel good," despite your knowing deep down inside that it was not a good idea of action.

Regardless, you convinced yourself that it was okay and even that it was not as bad as what other people did. Examples: Yes, I drive without a license but at least I got a permit. Yes I sleep with a married man or woman, but they aren't happy anyways. Yes, I gamble but I give a portion of my winnings to church. Yes, she's almost my daughter's age but she still is legal. Yes, I smoke marijuana at hookah bars but at least it's not crack cocaine in a crack house. Yes, I steal, lie, and cheat people sometimes, but I always ask God to forgive me right after.

Theses are all examples of what we do despite knowing that the "good" feelings will never truly satisfy us. As I have, we try to keep ungodly feelings hidden so that others don't see us as bad or distrustful people, so we just put on a daily front hoping it's never revealed. It's not just us ordinary folks who put on, but those of high position, such as politicians, pastors, professors, and celebrities. The truth was spoken about our two-sided mask in the book of Matthews 23;28 NIV: "In the same way, on the outside you appear to people as righteous but on the inside of you are full of hypocrisy and wickedness."

HEARING, SMELLING, TASTING, FEELING

There's always a day when it seems like nothing can really go wrong, and even if it tries to go wrong. You feel as though the strength of that positive energy can help you handle it. You say to yourself convincingly, "Today is that day that I claim whatever is missing in my life." It's a weekend yet you still feel a little restless from the busy work week that you barely physically made it through. You can't really fall asleep because, in your mind, that would be wasting a day when you could be celebrating. You start dialing up a few different friends or associates to see if they are going out. Something tells you to just stay home tonight, don't force tonight to happen; and yet, you make a call to that distant associate you don't really like, but is always down to hang out. You even go a step further to get in their car so they can drive, not really thinking clearly at that moment about the type of crowd that they regularly party with in their spare time.

The conversation you have is so much of a distraction that you don't bother to ask where you're headed to for the party. You finally get there and immediately see that this is not the particular spot you would've chosen.

But instead of going with your gut feeling and listening to that voice that's telling you to abort the whole mission in the first place, you decide to proceed inside. It's not like you haven't been at this location before, but that was a while ago when you were immature and just exploring life. In your mind, you pictured going to a nice chill lounge with good food and old school music, but instead, you end up at a hole-in-the-wall bar with all negative vibes, nasty-tasting food, and loud music. You order the "crash & burn" from the menu, which consists of cheap Murray's steakhouse wings that are covered in flaming hot sauce, so hot that it causes you to binge drink beer to cool your taste buds. The smell of the place reminds you of a high school locker room after a rainy football game, before the team has showered.

You still insist on staying to just let the night play out; besides, a part of you says over again, "Hey, I'm already out so what the heck," even though your gut says otherwise. Time passes by and everything seems to be going smooth so you think that this wasn't a bad idea after all. Then it starts: As you sit there trying to enjoy the moment, you can't help but to feel eyes staring at you, beaming on you like sun rays on a 96-degree summer day. You slowly turn around and lock eyes with someone you have never seen before and you can't figure out why he is staring. His expression is angry, like you owe him money or something.

You start to second guess your own mindset of thoughts: Maybe you know him and just can't remember. The individual walks up to where you and your associate are seated. You can't actually focus on what he is saying because your mind is still trying to rifle through your memory bank to figure out if the person is a past friend or enemy. You soon realize that he is more intoxicated than you are. An inner voice then whispers again, warning you to remove yourself from this setting now. But you ignore it once again, because the person has now walked away and you don't want to be the party by leaving early.

At this point, your thoughts of wisdom are battling with your emotional ego. You tell yourself that, even if things get out of hand with this unknown weirdo, there's enough security here to keep things from escalating. That would be a great assumption, but way deep down inside, you can feel that the lie you're telling yourself is going to actually play out the way you hope. Still, because you are scared of looking like a party pooper to your "friends," you convince yourself that you have no choice but to stay just a little while longer.

Meanwhile, the devilish plotting has begun for your demise. Eventually the lounge lets out for the night, and as the crowd pushes towards the exit, you spot the potential threat and hear his filthy, loud mouth. You try your best not to pay it any attention, yet the sounds get closer and closer to where you are, until you are staring at the guy in his face. Negative words are exchanged, even violent threats, which don't mix well with the grumpy, irritated crowd that's being pushed to exit the building. You realize though they're provoking you, and while you personally have the mental strength to ignore them, your associates are less tempered. So then it begins: The verbal back and forth shouting that eventually escalates into an all-out brawl between his crew and yours.

Ultimately, the fight is scattered away by security but it's too late: The person that had been antagonizing you is now lying on the cold concrete, not moving. He is bleeding from various locations of his body. Frantically, you remove yourself from the scene before the police arrive. Couple days go by and your conscience eats away at you. Then you see it: Your name and picture live on the news channel with an alert that you're now a wanted suspect after video clips surfaced from the lounge's surveillance footage.

It's all because of you! Don't ignore the God-given gift of you intuition and senses!

HIDDEN AGENDAS

I was asked one day, "How do you know for sure that you' become a man?" I answered, "When I was a child, I talked like a child, I thought like a child, I reasoned like a child. When I became a man, I put the ways of childhood behind me."

I know this statement is easier said than done, but to even begin that process, you have to perform a realistic, deep evaluation of the self. When doing this, most of us often just tackle surface problems that even other people can point out. But in order for you to really enhance yourself and mature, you must dig beyond the surface, where only you and God see your faults and the hidden agendas behind your actions.

Take myself for example: I was fighting a case for second degree assault and first degree attempted murder. My co-defendant was my younger cousin who I love and raised as a brother, which my lawyers realized after the state attorney presented numerous plea offers; they hoped that, because I was already in jail without a bail and my cousin was released on bail three months after his arrest, I would be persuaded to blame him. I denied all of their offers. Most lawyers are like politicians: They would say or do almost anything to keep the confidence of those who trust them to represent, even if that means to making unethical agreements with their opponents. Before trial, they used statements such as "If he compromises, he'll win the case and be a free man." Yes, it was true. I would've been free, but by compromising the way they wanted me to, I wouldn't have won at all. Even though my lawyer knew my loyalty to my cousin, it never stopped them from trying to convince me to do so, because the "win" would mainly benefit them. The states attorney would have a conviction, and my lawyer would have a defendant free, and yes, I would be physically free, but the possibility of someone I love suffering severely from lack of legal representation was mentally unacceptable. Realistically, I knew that, without my cousin having proper legal representation, they had enough evidence to give him at least twenty years of our maximum sentence of thirty years. I finally agreed to a guilty plea finishing, my time on home detention and three years of probation and my cousin with only three and half years, which had my lawyer and the state attorney puzzled since they knew that, had I pled not guilty, I would have won the case without a doubt due to lack of evidence on me.

Before I came home, I vowed to stay committed to God, waste as least time as possible, and to not have sex with anyone unless the woman was going to become my wife. In reality, it was hard as crap to control that desire, especially when I was locked up inside with a lot of time on my hands. Well, I got through three months and eventually gave in to my flesh. However, what I discovered was that I didn't find joy or satisfaction in the sex. I realized then that I needed to truly do some soul-searching and try to figure out my relationship to sex.

The more I searched my soul, I realized that I just wasn't spiritually or emotionally attracted to the woman I had been with, nor was I to those women in the past. Unlike a "gold digger," I was more of a gold collector who just dug deep in the minds of women until they released their mental treasures. I never was a fan of expecting things like money, jewelry, expensive gifts, and paid bills. My biological dad used to tell me, "Everybody uses everybody, but it's how you use someone that determines what type of person you are."

Instead, in my "gold collecting," I aimed for something deeper than any tangible gift. I yearned for the gold that the average man probably cared less about. While others thought of master strategies to get into a woman's panties, I focused on getting their treasure of belief, trust, and ultimately love. Some men also use those targets as methods to get sex. For me, sex was the easiest part of men and women; the relationship is the hard part. Most women now seem to be more demanding, yet their self-image and standards are lower, not only with younger ladies but also with older ones. Older women seem to date men as if they're in a competition with younger women, especially when dating younger men. As for younger women, many have not been passed down strong values from the older generation, so many resort to getting a man through sex, instead of preserving their full worth.

So then, you have a guy like myself who is coming from an old school mindset that women often call "complicated." A wise man once told me that my method of dating was a gift and a curse, a statement I didn't get it until I got older and matured. The gift is that, when I meet people, especially women, I look further than their surface and see their potential. For example, some people come off arrogant with a snappy attitude, but I can see that it's a wall to protect the soft, sensitive inner emotion that had been damaged by life inside the ghetto. Some women act as if they don't want a man, but they might be hiding the fact that they don't even know what a real man looks like if God Himself handed them one Himself, only because they didn't have their dad or father figure around as an example of how a real man should present himself.

Now, the "curse," on the other hand, is that, despite your seeing their potential, people are often convinced that they are who they portray. The person who comes off snappy and arrogant is fine with exactly what you see. Those who say they don't want a man have convinced themselves of that statement and go so far as to date someone of their same sex to try and prove themselves, which ignores what is written in the book of Leviticus 18:22: "You shall not lie with a male as one lies with a female, it's an abomination." Then, you have women with ghetto mentalities and, even though you can see great potential in them, they are content with themselves being products of their environment.

I too grew up in the ghetto and saw firsthand what goes on. But after a while, I grew to mature and I learned that there are two types of people that are in the ghetto: The one that lives in the ghetto and the ones that live ghetto. The one who just happened to live there and take up opportunities to actively remove themselves are the ones to keep around, because their environment doesn't dictate their drive for better. The ones who are ghetto are content with their circumstances and, even if you show them a better way of living, they are more likely to bring you to their environmental lifestyle, which will ultimately bring you down. If you cannot see who you surround yourself with because you are blinded by lust and pleasure, you have already lost yourself in their world. The funny part is that most folks step back and realize that the person they are with is not right or functional, yet they stay yoked for their own selfish agendas.

Within time, you learn that everyone has agendas in life, especially when dealing with others—some are good and some are not so good. The golden rule is to treat others as you want to be treated, but life teaches us that some just have bad agenda with no regards of how their actions might affect you. Many people you going to meet and even those around you presently have connected with you because of who you are, something you have, or what you can do. Their agendas vary: They may want you for protection, popularity, business, wealth, wingman/woman, recreation, etc. Some come to you and love you, yes, but before anyone can love you, they must first have a motive to begin liking you. Whatever the reasons, through your God given instincts and maturity, now your choice to allow certain people more access to your life or separate yourself to prevent them from negatively affecting you and those you love.

DEDICATION

The utmost Praise to God, Yahweh, for the sacrifice of His son Jesus the Christ, Yeshua, who allowed my repentance to be valid. Without it, I am not possible.

Second, I want to thank God for my #1 supporter, my helpmate, my friend, and my Rib, Kristin, for her constant gentleness support. My two princesses, Makenze Patterson aka Chipmunk who was my first inspiration to live a better life and Audriana Blackledge aka Little One for all the hugs you ask daddy for, even on days I had nothing to laugh or smile about.

Antionette "Niecy" Williams, my hero who showed me what faith is: With God's mercy and grace, you defeated an obstacle that doctors said would kill you within three months, but, eight years later, you are still alive and singing your favorite song, "Devil, God's Not Done With Me Yet."

The elders of the family, my grandparents Eddie and Linda Williams. Thanks for teaching me the proper structure of family and being vessels of God. Grandma Marva "Cookie" Queen, thank you for being the root of my tough side and loving me the best way you could. Grandmother-in-Law, Victoria Merritt, thank you for being the first to completely accept me as new family through your pure spirit of Godly love.

Earl "The Mailman" Minter: There are not enough words to express the gratitude that runs through me, for being my reintroduction to the path of Christ, for being my first prison visitor without the "I told you so" comment, for giving me the opportunity on 106.1FM Radio One, for being the first real author of a book that I know, and for always being a mentor and father figure. I am truly humbled to have you on my team.

Major love to my first prison ministry church and brothers: Christ Pastor Kendrick Boyd, Rodje "Voyce" Williams, Robert "King Africa" Quanza, Tory "Moody" Gamble, and all those still inside at Hagerstown Maryland correctional facility. "It ain't no use of nobody trying to turn us around. No, no."

Thank you to my brothers by blood and action— Xavier Hawkins, William Campbell, Adolfo Lucas, Paul Dinkins, Lonnie "Bo" Byrd, Breye Chesley, Andrew Stanford, Rashid Smith, John Gould, Damien Patterson, Shelton Lowery, and Kenard Eubanks—for allowing me to learn and grow from you all.

Elder Stan and Aunt Debbie, thank you for the best inspirational married couple session that constantly helps my family build a better bond and union.

Many thanks to Kimberly Lowery (the female version of me), Jonelle M. Williams (my twin), Maurice Williams, Maurice Williams Jr., Chynthia Casey (third mom), Destiny (mopay/first daughter) Grant, Paisly Simmons, Keniya Eubanks, Lamika Winfree (love you regardless of how far you live), Ceara Williams, Mya Williams, Maurice Lowery, Kendrick Lowery, Malik Williams, Lil Xavier Hawkins, Eric Williams, Eddie (Lil Eddie) Williams, Jamal Simmons, Calvin (DJ Twisted Thompson, Marvin Williams, Damonte, John, and Melvin (Man Mugg) Gould, Uncles Marquise (Key-Z-Mooe), Marvin Williams Jr., Stephone Williams, and Eddie Jr. "Kato" Willams.

Thanks also to all my non-believers of Jesus Christ, for you are one of my biggest inspirations that dared me to go at God 100% through actions, so that you too can now hopefully believe the power of God and finally accept Jesus as your Lord and Savior.

My dear friend, Checkeria Lacy, who is my family's greatest supporter. I'm blessed that you knew me less than most people, yet believed in me more.

RIP Charlotte "Sherry" Williams: I know you are in heaven saying, "You go, boy!" Oh, how you played a major role in my life. Love you always.

I appreciate everyone who took a moment out of their time to listen to my story. I sincerely apologize to all those who I have allowed my deeply rooted past to hurt during my journey, whether mentally, emotionally, spiritually, or physically. Regardless if you were meant to be in my life for a reason, season, or lifetime, I am humbly grateful for our experiences that helped pull me from my addiction to lies within and ultimately groomed the strength I stand with today.

POEMS

Terrell Patterson

A GROWING ROSE

She has great potential, yes, a little work
Is needed but how can I help her,
Her ex-Boyfriend has her feelings nearly frozen
Got me thinking how can I melt her?

Can't say I really believe in love at first sight
But if the sight of her got me feeling this way
I want her and certainly she's worth the fight.

I would cherish a woman with her great style
Ride it to the wheels fall off, to God here's my hand
Not to belittle dude before me, she just deserves a
better man.

It's not my style to hate on a player
Maybe I disapprove of the games he play
It's for the wrong person, just pass the controller this way.

It bothers me that the joy I can give her
She really wishes it was from him
Don't matter if I'm better for her, if for him there's no end.

It's like my time is all hers his time is elsewhere
Yet still it's him her focus is given to,
Emotionally pushing me away, so when do I say
I'm through?

Addicted to Lies

It's too early to throw in the tile
Deciding on him or me for her is painful,
Hurt blinding her to recognize a good man
Who desires to be her guardian Angel.

Funny how we chase love in the direction of LUST
Yearning for what isn't mine shows God I lack TRUST,
He gave stability in situation, yet still I FUSS.
I asked for love, He said "why aren't I ENOUGH!

TEARLESS CRIES

Who will cry for me and the pain that I'm facing?
Who will cry when I fall running after dreams I'm chasing?
Who will cry when Adversity hits me from every Angle?
Who will cry and come to my rescue hopefully my
guardian Angel?
Who will cry as disasters strikes my life like a hurricane
Katrina?
Who will cry when I'm the New Orleans un-helped by
Project FEMA?
Who will cry if my household crumbles from being planted
in the wrong soil?
Who will cry with the same lack of tears from fish dying
because oceans polluted with oil?
Who will cry tears of Joy when God bless my wife and I to
walk that aisle?
Who will cry tears of Hope when my freedom hangs on
court trial?
Who will cry loud enough convincing others for me
to listen?
Who will cry only to brag you cried or only a competition?
Who will cry Help! Help! to provide for my children?
Who will cry that desperate need or will they all sail off like
pilgrims?
Who will cry that cry that not even Jesus Christ can hear?
Who will cry that empty cry is the only cry I fear?

Untitled

Hurt people, hurt people, but why?
They beat the problem, yet don't seek aid for the pain,
Feeling immune to dark clouds,
Still no shelter when it rains.
I'm good, I got it, convinced yourself,
Wisdom said, your only human,
God's doing CPR, hurt is destroying your health.
Love came, 2 love you as an equal,
Pain was a gun, love was the target,
Why? Because, hurt people, hurt people.
Walking dead, w/o deceased odors,
Searching for Mr. or Mrs. "Right",
In return Mr./Mrs. "Wrong" leftovers.
Be real, self-love is Not in people,
God 1st, and real love will follow,
Meantime. Hurt people will only attract hurt people.

ABOUT THE AUTHOR

Terrell Patterson is an author, businessman, speaker, husband, and father of two. A native of Baltimore City, Patterson has overcome the many obstacles of growing up in a fast-paced and high-risk environment, including the loss of family members, abandonment from his parents, street violence, and drugs. With his experience and knowledge, he now empowers others through delivering the Word of God and sharing his testimony, a purpose he re-discovered while mentoring over thirty inmates in a maximum security prison.

Patterson currently remains in Baltimore City with his wife and two daughters. When he is not writing, he enjoys working out, playing sports, traveling, and performing spoken word poetry.

CREATING DISTINCTIVE BOOKS
WITH INTENTIONAL RESULTS

We're a collaborative group of creative masterminds
with a mission to produce high-quality books to position
you for monumental success in the marketplace.

Our professional team of writers, editors, designers,
and marketing strategists work closely together to ensure
that every detail of your book is a clear representation
of the message in your writing.

Want to know more?
Write to us at info@publishyourgift.com
or call (888) 949-6228

Discover great books, exclusive offers, and more at
www.PublishYourGift.com

Connect with us on social media

@publishyourgift